COUNTING ON DEATH

A Marine Infantryman's Journey from the Front Lines of Combat to the Fight for Peace

JOSHUA SHORES

CASEMATE
Pennsylvania & Yorkshire

Published in the United States of America and Great Britain in 2025 by
CASEMATE PUBLISHERS
1950 Lawrence Road, Havertown, PA 19083
and
47 Church Street, Barnsley, S70 2AS, UK

Hardcover Edition: ISBN 978-1-63624-570-6
Digital Edition: ISBN 978-1-63624-571-3

A CIP record for this book is available from the British Library

Printed and bound in the United States of America by Integrated Books International

Typeset in India by Lapiz Digital Services, Chennai.

For a complete list of Casemate titles, please contact:

CASEMATE PUBLISHERS (US)
Telephone (610) 853-9131
Fax (610) 853-9146
Email: casemate@casematepublishers.com
www.casematepublishers.com

CASEMATE PUBLISHERS (UK)
Telephone (0)1226 734350
Email: casemate@casemateuk.com
www.casemateuk.com

Contents

To all of the Gold Star families, I am sorry for your loss.

To the members of 1st Battalion, 5th Marine Regiment
who were killed in action in Ramadi:

Alpha Company
Corporal K. Matthew Cannan
Lance Corporal Johnathan R. Flores
Corporal Jesse Jamie
Lance Corporal Chad B. Maynard
Lance Corporal Marty G. Mortenson
Corporal Tyler S. Trovillian
Lance Corporal Dion M. Whitley

Bravo Company
Captain James C. Edge
Corporal Jeffrey B. Starr
Lance Corporal Adam J. Strain

Charlie Company
Staff Sergeant Ramon E. Gonzalez
Lance Corporal Erik R. Heldt
Captain John W. Maloney

Weapons Company
Lance Corporal Evenor C. Herrera
Corporal Garry W. Rimes

Headquarters and Support Company
Petty Officer Second Class Cesar O. Baez

And to the several other men who have taken their
own lives since our deployment.

Acknowledgments

Thank you to the person who has stayed by me through thick and thin, who has had to endure the long nights of my tossing and turning and struggles with coping, has encouraged me to take risks, and who I look forward to sharing the rest of my days with: my wife. I love you.

Thank you to my two wonderful kids who give me a reason to live and whose existence has saved me more times than you'll ever know. You are amazing and I love you.

Thank you to Doctors Laura and Dona. Without your help I'd be dead.

Thank you to all who have supported me in this writing.

Thank you to my friends and family who have put up with me and my sometimes difficult-to-understand personality over the years.

Thank you to Ken and Ruth, Kelly, Erik, Lisa, David, Andy, and Joan.

Thank you to all the Marines, sailors, and other coalition forces I served alongside and for those who continue to serve.

For more information about the Marines and sailors of 1st Battalion, 5th Marine Regiment, please visit https://1stbattalion5thmarinesassociation.com/.

Foreword

This is not a war story. This is written by Joshua Shores to provide insight on the nature of combat as he experienced it and share his memories. The book has been a work he began shortly after his time in the Marine Corps infantry and specifically focuses on his time in Alpha Company, 1st Battalion, 5th Marine Regiment (A 1/5) in the city of Ramadi, Iraq, in 2005. The following memoir is not an effort to document historical events but rather to tell his story.

Joshua served as an infantry combat Marine during the War on Terror, graduating from boot camp as a meritorious private first class and transitioning as a staff sergeant after tours of duty to Iraq and Afghanistan. He served in an extremely intense and dynamic tour in Ramadi, where he participated in an unimaginable level of combat.

I was the company commander for A 1/5 during the author's Ramadi tour of duty. He was my Marine. I am an eyewitness to much of Josh's narrative. It is difficult to describe the amount of combat A 1/5 saw in Ramadi. Virtually every Marine was wounded in some fashion. As such, many didn't think (or know) to report wounds as they didn't feel deserving of a Purple Heart medal given so many others had been killed or gravely wounded. At the time, also, there was conjecture as to what wounds rated a Purple Heart, such as blast wounds and concussions. Josh would receive a Purple Heart 18 years after returning from Ramadi.

I served in the Marine Corps for the better part of 30 years both as an enlisted infantry Marine and officer. Everything I experienced, through training, intense deployments, and combat led me to being the company commander of A 1/5 in Ramadi in 2005. I do not have to reflect as I continue to live that time every day and through dreams. I have come to embrace all of it and yet I find I have no one to share it with. This memoir is truly exceptional to me as it is a shared experience. Josh and I were separated by what he saw and experienced and what I saw and experienced even though we were in the same unit, at the same time, and saw each other near daily; he has asked me to elaborate.

For context, I had fought with Alpha Company in Fallujah, Iraq, the year before and was with many of the same men in the battalion when we returned. Only 17 percent of the Marine Corps consists of infantry and, because of that, more than thirty percent of us in our unit would be on our third combat tour. These were not deployments. These were combat tours. One of the principal aspects I know about Marines is that we do not seek to cause harm but are often forced into it. After the initial invasion of Iraq in 2003, our unit was assigned to Al Anbar province to provide stability and security operations. When four contractors were killed and hung from a bridge after being lit on fire in Fallujah, everything changed. We were ordered to close with and destroy the enemy that conducted this atrocity, and we did just that. Politics fueled by global media would intervene, creating a cease-fire of sorts, but the fighting would continue in Al Anbar regardless. Eventually we would rotate back to the United States, being replaced by Marine units that would be called upon to finish the destruction of the enemy in Fallujah with more deliberate military planning and a conservative approach to media involvement.

While back in the States, we continued to train for our imminent return to Iraq. This involved the basics of shoot, move, and communicate—essentially closing with and destroying the enemy through fire and close combat, task and purpose orders succinctly, and increased combat-aid training for all Marines. Gone, at that time, were uniform inspections, administrative nonsense, and activities that had nothing to do with the future task at hand.

There is a human, family, aspect to all this. We all knew some of us would not be coming back from our next tour. I was acutely aware of this responsibility as company commander. Maximum liberty was granted as appropriate although rare due to the intense training. I had occasional conversations with fellow Marines who believed they would not survive the next one. Many of us did not think we would survive yet again. Many of us did not. When the time came, every one of us got on that bus to be transferred to the air base from where we would fly back to possible death or dismemberment. We all went back. Those who survived were never the same.

I will tell the reader that it is not just the experience in country and in combat. It is the before, the after, and the enduring effects it has on you and everyone around you. Yes, each of us manage in our own way but who we are now affects loved ones and friends. It is who we have become. I believe Josh's story is about who we have become and who we aspire to be.

Josh began this journey of producing a memoir focused on personal therapy. Along the way he examines the nature of the human condition associated with combat and how it affects him. The reader will find the story to be brutally honest and will come away with an understanding of Josh's quest for a purpose-filled life of grace and forgiveness.

Kelsey R. Thompson Lt. Col., USMC (Ret.)

Introduction

This story is mine alone. It is not an attempt to tell the story of anyone else I've served with as we view each of our accounts of events through a different lens. It is not a memoir written in an attempt to brag or gain notoriety (naturally, the Navy SEALs take the lead for that type). This is a work of creative nonfiction. I have portrayed the events to the best of my recollections. While all the stories in this book are true, I changed some names and identifying details to protect the privacy of the people involved. I have tried to recreate events, locales, and conversations from memory.

I've felt compelled to tell my story from Ramadi as it documents my life as a 19-year-old Marine. Though the choices I made reflect on the Marine Corps, because I am a Marine, my hope in writing this memoir is to shed light on the true nature of war. After watching online videos of the brutal combat in Ukraine and Israel, and comparing them to my own experiences, I realize we can do so much better. In early 2025, after I returned from observing drone warfare in Kharkiv and Izyum in Ukraine, my heart broke for the young men and women who were on the front lines. If they are fortunate enough to survive, the decisions they made while fighting will either give them peace or haunt them. We can do better as individuals, as military units, and as citizens to refrain from making the same mistakes that repeatedly seem to rear their ugly head in war. As I matured in the Marines and attended leadership schools, I learned what it was to be a genuine leader. As a junior Marine on my first deployment, I was thrown to the wolves. Marines who had twice been to combat in Iraq surrounded me. Because of the deployment tempo, many had missed the opportunity to attend leadership schools. I'm not blaming anyone for my own decisions. Some of the combat veterans had their own interpretation of what leadership meant, and those ideas influenced some behaviors I believed were acceptable in combat. I spent the rest of my time in the Marine Corps working to earn a position as a leader as I didn't want my junior Marines to have to carry the weight of decisions as I did. I'd like to think I was successful, but only those who served in combat with me, under my direction in Afghanistan, can attest to how successful I truly was in these attempts of redemption.

This is the story of one person, one squad, one platoon, one company, and one battalion. I know other men and women out there have had worse experiences than mine. My purpose here is not to compare stories but simply to tell my own, specifically, the story of my time in Iraq and how it changed me as a person. It changed my very soul. Serving in the armed forces, especially the Marine Corps, is something I am proud of and would not want to change. Unfortunately, I cannot rewind the past and change decisions that were made; I would if I could. For my brothers reading this, I hope you understand why I needed to write this memoir. I hope it does not disappoint you and, if you feel similarly, I hope it brings you some sense of relief in knowing you're not alone.

One of our comrades who read this memoir in draft form made a comment that has stuck with me. He said, "This is not your story to tell." I didn't know what to think of that comment. My initial reaction was hurt and anger. Publishing it after that feedback made me feel like a narcissist. After years of reflection, I decided it was my story to tell after all. The situations in the memoir are raw and unfiltered. I don't write about them because I am proud of all of them, but I wanted to bring them to light to show that anyone is susceptible to change. The events in the memoir are those I've experienced directly and heard from people who were present. I understand why the Marine was upset after reading this memoir, specifically about the event I suspect he felt was his or someone else's, not mine, to share. However, that event also affected me. War leaves an impact on every person who takes part in it. The events in Iraq will haunt me until the day I die. The decisions I made and the unanswered questions surrounding them haunt me every morning when I wake up.

Families and friends back home were proud of us.

"Go kill 'em boys!" our friends would say.

"Kill those scumbags!" our relatives would say.

We did just that. With those actions, I've come to realize we shouldn't encourage killing among men or expect those who do will be able to easily slide back into society. Our society teaches us the differences between good and evil, yet we all talk about how easy it would be to take a life. We fantasize about being warriors. Our current culture of becoming a "warrior" in all walks of life encourages it. Businessmen attend corporate retreats to experience building a combat brotherhood. To be men, to kill. We don't need encouragement for that; that drive is already part of our complicated psyche. War only serves to open the gates to an unbelievable hell our complex human brains create; so complex that only we, as humans, can come up with new and brutal ways to maim and dismember fellow humans. We are among the only beings on earth who use our brains to create new ways to torture our own kind.

This memoir is the story of what happens when no one is watching, when men have nothing to hold back their genuine emotions. This is war. These are the things that need to be discussed so they may not happen again. As Americans, we cannot deny these events happened. It is ignorant to think American military members can overcome the animalistic behavior that results from the stresses of combat. We do not differ from any other military or terrorist organization when it comes down to our reactions to stressful situations. We just have the laws of the United States and our allies to abide by. Marines are humans first and we are capable of both great and terrible things. We bleed, we mourn, we hurt, we react, and, later, we regret.

There are many people I wish I could apologize to, many actions I wish I could take back. We turned into monsters, into the enemy, a terrorist to a different country. We became who we were fighting and the civilians of Ramadi paid for it. To them, I am sorry. I hope this memoir can lead at least one Marine, sailor, or soldier to make better decisions and learn from our mistakes.

Some of these chapters may be difficult and uncomfortable to read. But remember, these are the horrors that we combat veterans ruminate on for the rest of our lives. I'm not seeking sympathy for any of the things I have done or have happened. I believe in karma and I believe the struggles I have with my life stem from some decisions I made while in Iraq. Skipping parts, or choosing not to be present was not a luxury we had while in combat. We lived through it without the convenience of skipping sections or chapters. We did our best and, at times, floundered. Some events that occurred in Ramadi were so close to the line of right and wrong that I left those events alone for God to judge, not the reader (all is fair in love and war). For those I served with, I am grateful we fought together to get each other home.

I begrudgingly came back to writing this memoir after having read many history books on warfare and political policies over the past decade. I wish I had been more interested in reading the memoirs and history of battle prior to my deployments so I could better understand what combat truly was. The Commandant's Reading List isn't just for skimming over; it's meant to be a foundation to survive the mental and physical demands of combat. Boot camp only scratches the surface of combat readiness; I wish someone had informed me about it before throwing me into the wolf's den. For the longest time, I was ashamed of my service in Ramadi and some decisions I had made. It wasn't until I had read several books on war and psychology that I began my journey of healing.

It was in the psychology genre that I eventually found solace in having been in war. The 1971 Stanford Prison Experiment paved the path of forgiveness for me. Because of the changes that occurred with the participants and their roles, the experiment, which was supposed to last two weeks, only lasted six days. The researchers randomly assigned college students roles as prisoner or jailer, expecting them to behave accordingly. The experiment revealed that abuses of power and authority can affect anyone, regardless of their background or self-identification. I experienced this firsthand as a naive teenager with the backing of the United States military.

If you're currently serving in the armed forces, educate yourself. We owe it to our nation to represent ourselves better than our enemies. If you're an officer or noncommissioned officer, you owe it to the Marines or soldiers in your care. Anton Myrer, a former corporal in the Marine

Corps, wrote *Once an Eagle*, widely considered one of the best novels on life as an officer in the military. The power of such influence from an enlisted man, to write a novel that inspires leadership from all ranks for one of the best combat forces in the world, demonstrates it's the person behind the rank who can influence change in our world.

I've noticed a doubt that exists in people regarding veterans' struggles with mental health, as if we veterans have to be wearing our struggle on our sleeve to prove the amount of damage we carry. I know there are people who are of similar mind to me who are one bullet away from ending their life. As a veteran and Marine, I carry the pride of my service and would never wish to bring another comrade down with my troubles. The struggle we endure with our mental health is that we don't want to bring the devil into other people's lives. We battle our demons in silence, with what we believe to be honor, so as not to disturb others with our troubles. From my experience, I believe this is why we see so many veteran suicides.

Unfortunately, I get it. From the perspective of a combatant and someone who has attempted suicide, that option can feel like the only one. Nobody, especially veterans, likes to show weakness. We tightly rein in our thoughts and emotions, putting our best foot forward for the outside world, until we can no longer bear the burden. Suicide often seems like the best option to deal with this overwhelming burden and avoid putting further stress on those around us. For those of us who have taken a life and know how easy the action of it is, what's one more? But we can do better. We can reach out to talk to those we served with. We have a national duty and obligation to care for the ones who made it home so we can properly honor those who made the ultimate sacrifice. Those of us who survived were left feeling disappointed as we were counting on death, only to be spared to live a life burdened with the actions and memories of war.

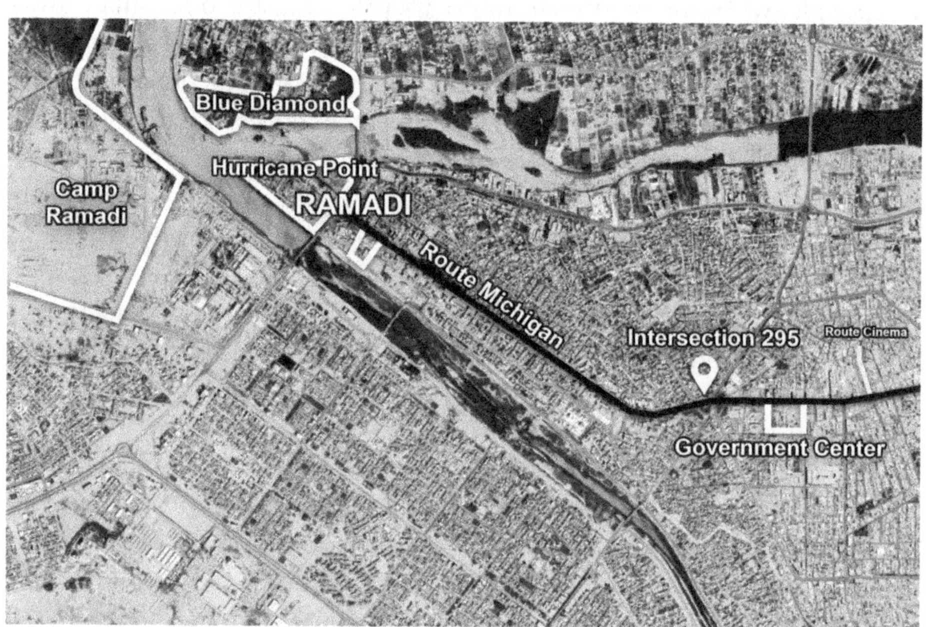

Map of Ramadi showing key routes and Alpha Company forward operating bases. (Map Data: Google, Airbus)

CHAPTER I

The Road to War

Growing Up

My upbringing as a God-fearing, Lutheran-raised, small-town kid took place in Wisconsin. Overall, my childhood experiences and quality of life were great. Throughout high school, I never committed to subscribing to a label because I had friends in many different social groups. Working hard was something embedded in my persona; my first job at the age of ten was helping my dad prepare metal parts for finishing. During one period in high school, I juggled four jobs while still making time for my girlfriend. Looking back, I can say I lived a great young life and was naive about how the world outside of my small town operated.

I knew I wanted to be a Marine ever since I was a young boy, probably around twelve years old. I would see my family members' military photos when I'd visit their homes and enjoyed perusing my father's photos from when he served. Running around my yard, dressed in my father's old Marine combat utilities, I loved shooting at my friends with the makeshift guns we created from toys or sticks. The challenges of serving in the military and the honor I felt came with that, having looked up to my family members, made the decision easy for me. When I told my dad I wanted to be a Marine, he asked me to consider some of the other branches, just to see what they might offer. He also told me he would pay my way through college should I choose that route. My father never pressured me either way and left the decision entirely up to me. He attempted to explain to me what the Marine Corps was like; however, armed with the arrogance of youth, I felt I knew better.

On September 10, 2001, I was sitting in my sophomore high school art class and wanted to make a drawing of a sniper. My art teacher didn't want me to create a drawing without it having some meaning to me. I told her I had always wanted to be a Marine, but she tried to encourage me to venture outside of my comfort zone. Class ended and I left to contemplate what I should make for a piece of art. The following day, on September 11, the reason to create my drawing became crystal clear. I drew an image of a sniper overlaying the flag of Afghanistan. My teacher never asked me again why I drew that image. It was obvious, even to the liberal woman teaching high school art: we needed to kill terrorists.

At the age of 17, my parents had to sign for my enlistment into the Marine Corps' Delayed Entry Program (DEP). My mom cried when she signed the papers; I assured her it was better for me to get some experience in the DEP prior to departing for boot camp, as I would enlist anyway when I turned 18. I was so excited to get on with my life from high school that I made sure to pack all of the required high school classes my junior and senior year so I could graduate early and go to boot camp in February having just turned 18 the prior fall.

Boot camp was just like most movies and books describe. It's amusing to read books like Robert Leckie's *Helmet for my Pillow* and appreciate the similarities of Marine recruit training from the 1940s to my experiences; not much had changed. Despite being one of the youngest recruits in my platoon, I made my way up to squad leader roughly halfway through boot camp. I was determined to make it to the end, though it was the most difficult thing I had been through at that point in my life. My girlfriend from high school wrote to me often, and I held on to the thought of our life together once I was done with boot camp. I graduated boot camp as a private first class and traveled home on leave, ready to move to the School of Infantry (SOI) afterward.

When I enlisted, the recruiters promised my parents I'd be able to walk across the stage to receive my high school diploma, even if I had already graduated boot camp. The recruiters reassured me and my parents that my February boot camp date would line up perfectly with my boot leave so I could attend my high school graduation. They lied. My dad had to go to the recruiter's office and "have a talk" with them, as I was awaiting orders to return to Camp Pendleton, California. I don't know how he did it, but he had me assigned to recruiter's assistance, where I was to help the local recruiters work our area, so I could walk and receive my diploma. When it came time for the graduation ceremony, the principal of the high school asked if I had picked up my gown from the office during our rehearsal the night before. I told him I had planned on wearing my dress blues for the ceremony. He told me he wanted me to wear my gown, as he didn't want anyone to be different. I acknowledged him and showed up the next evening wearing my dress blues. When he saw me, he said, "Oh, you wore that?" as he looked me up and down, with a hint of disgust on his face. I told him I had earned it and I was going to wear my blues. I walked across the stage, received my diploma, and unexpectedly received a standing ovation from the crowd. Afterward, my peers and their families congratulated me on completing boot camp and wished me luck on my future time as a Marine infantryman. So many people hoped I would go "over there" and kill as many terrorists as I could. Or they'd say, "Kill them for God!" If only they really knew what they were truly asking me to do and what I was promising I'd do for them. I'm a man of my word and I felt an obligation and duty to uphold my promises.

After I completed the graduation festivities, I packed my seabag and departed for California. When my flight landed, I went to the USO (United Service Organizations) in the airport to change my clothes. I had to get into my Alpha uniform to check in to the SOI. The extra week I'd had on recruiter's assistance at home did me no favors; when I went to button my Alpha jacket, it was as though I were squeezing into someone else's clothes. The jacket fit a skinnier version of me. I had gained 15 pounds while on leave and looked like a bag of smashed assholes as I checked into my training. It was time to train to kill the terrorists and get back into shape.

Boot

After graduating from the SOI, I tried out to become a Reconnaissance Marine and was selected. I was assigned to the 1st Reconnaissance Battalion for a two-month period and began the training to be sent to the Basic Reconnaissance Course (Recon). After being with Recon for one month, I decided I wasn't ready to be a Recon Marine. I was tired of being treated like a recruit all over again, and I was concerned I would miss out on the war. I had overheard many Recon Marines talking of the year-and-a-half it took to become one of them and, being an impatient 18-year-old, I did not want to spend all my time training and not being able to use the skills I had developed. After understanding more of what the training involved and seeing how long the war lasted, I do sometimes wish I hadn't quit, but I would not be the person I am today had I not.

I was extremely excited to learn I would go to the 1st Battalion, 5th Marine Regiment (1/5). After taking part in the 2003 invasion of Iraq and fighting in Fallujah, the regiment was preparing to deploy to the capital of the Anbar Province, Ramadi, from March 2005. One of the members of the cadre at the training course mentioned the battles within the so-called Triangle of Death and informed us we would most likely be sent there from 1st Recon Battalion. As a naive teenager, I was finally getting my wish.

I was assigned to Alpha Company, 1/5. For a lot of the guys in my battalion, this would be their third deployment to Iraq. We were one of two battalions that had these back-to-back combat deployments. The focus of my predeployment training when I arrived at 1/5 was on the effective killing of the enemy and handling of personnel under control (PUC). I furthered my education on how to kill people effectively using a rifle, shotgun, grenades, and numerous other explosive devices. Upon my arrival at 1st Platoon, someone reminded me of the proper way to fire a burst with the M249 Squad Automatic Weapon (SAW). Shouting "Die, motherfucker, die!" allowed for the appropriate amount of time to pull the trigger for an effective six- to eight-round burst of linked 5.56 full-metal-jacket rounds to fly downrange. Our training taught us to be wary of most people we would come in contact with as they might be hiding something and couldn't be trusted. During all of our company and battalion exercises, we focused on extracting information from the locals; the people who were role-players, usually just Marines dressed up like civilians, always had valuable information. We never handed out candy to children or smiled and waved to any of the role-players. That would have seemed absurd, but we should have been doing that; if only we knew the consequences of only preparing to kill in the long-term outlook on the War on Terror.

Many of the junior enlisted Marines who were our newer leaders didn't have the chance to go to advanced leadership training because of the deployment tempo. They learned from their superiors on previous deployments. They followed in the footsteps of those before them; I mimicked their behavior and followed their orders accordingly. That's what Marines do. Our senior lance corporals and corporals told us new arrivals, or "boots," stories of combat in Fallujah and during the initial invasion. The first casualty of the Iraq war was Lieutenant Childers, of Alpha Company, 1/5. Several Marines had served alongside him and made it known we were just replacements for the warriors who died before us. We had a lot to live up to; our senior Marines made sure we knew it.

Our training focused on fighting a war, not how to police a population. It would come as a surprise to all of us when we arrived in Iraq and were told our new mission was to win over the "hearts and minds" of the population. We were training to level the city, to fight for our country. What we didn't prepare for was working to protect the civilians, which would prove to be an arduous task to accomplish when we arrived in Ramadi. The city had a population of around 300,000. We had heard stories about the 2nd Battalion, 4th Marine Regiment (2/4) and 2nd Battalion, 5th Marine Regiment (2/5) in Ramadi that mainly described their losses. We were going to be relieving 2/5. It seemed to me things should have been slowing down after having two battalions in the city. I thought casualties would be minimal and that, overall, it would be a cultural experience with some small firefights here and there. Even when we sat down and listened to our battalion commander give a speech about our upcoming deployment, I didn't believe it would be anything bad. Even after he guaranteed us that not everyone would come home alive, I refused to believe we could die. I felt we were too well trained, too capable, for anything bad to happen. I was so naive.

During the months leading up to the deployment, my attitude began to change. Following a breakup with my girlfriend, I began dating a married woman. I drank a lot and maxed out my credit card. I didn't care about anyone else. My only desire was to be happy and do what I wanted to do. I felt obligated to act irresponsibly and live on the edge. I wanted to feel as much of life as I could before going to war.

Over my predeployment leave, I slept with three different girls, broke up with the married woman, and got back together with my high school sweetheart. I hosted a bunch of parties at my parents' house where my friends, family, and I were all able to say goodbye. One night, when my friends were being loud in my parents' basement, my dad called me to the top of the stairs. After just a few drinks, I was thoroughly enjoying my evening.

My dad was an infantry Marine in the late 1970s. His father and grandfather both served in the Army in both world wars. He is a very stern, honest, and hardworking man. All my friends respected and feared him. He would give you the shirt off his back and could always be counted on to point you in the right direction. The thing is, you just never wanted to upset him. He's a big guy like me. He stands at six foot four and is a sizable man. When he talks, people listen. When he yells, I've seen him make men cry. I love my dad and that's why it bothered me, my entire deployment in Ramadi, when I couldn't say sorry for what I said that night.

He greeted me at the top of the stairs in his boxers. He stood tall and authoritative when he told me in his low, slow, direct voice, "Josh, everyone needs to leave. Now." His deep voice cut through the sound of the party.

I knew both he and my mom had to work the next morning and needed the rest, but I didn't care. I was having a good time with friends that I didn't think I was going to see again.

"Dad," I said sternly. Our eyes locked. "Go the fuck to bed."

I had never seen my dad's eyes look like they did after those words left my mouth. Pain seemed to overwhelm him. His posture dropped, and he looked at the floor. I stood my ground, tall and foolishly confident. He turned from me and returned to bed. I walked downstairs and wondered why I had said that to the person I most respected. I immediately felt ashamed, but my own selfish pride allowed my feet to step down the remaining steps. It was the first time I had ever said anything like that to my dad, and it was the first time I saw him defeated. I didn't like it, yet I didn't have the courage to tell him I was sorry. I so badly wanted to apologize before I left the airport terminal to leave for war, but I couldn't utter the words "I'm sorry"—two simple words I regretted not saying to my dad the whole time I was in Iraq. It was one of the first things he and I discussed when I returned. I told him I was sorry how I had responded the night before I left. To him, I don't think it was that big of a deal. He was happy I had made it home safe. His reaction, to me, meant the world.

The Trip Over

The plane ride to Kuwait was terrible. We were on a commercial flight and a Marine occupied every seat. The seats were filled with not only men but also weapons, body armor, and helmets, all of which we were required to carry on the flight. I'm six feet seven inches tall. With my body armor, Kevlar helmet, and M249 SAW beneath my feet for the 19-hour flight, I felt more than a little cramped. On top of being uncomfortable, the flight crew thought it would be a great idea to show movies like *Ladder 49*, a film about a firefighter who becomes trapped in a horrific blaze. This would be like showing *The Green Mile* to someone on death row. The only good things about the flight were the beautiful flight attendants and the hot towels for wiping the grease-like sweat from our faces. I never traveled much by air growing up and had never had a hot towel given to me. It took my having to go to war to experience that one last comfort of the First World.

We arrived in Kuwait early in the morning. I walked off the plane and immediately felt the dry desert air against my stale and sweaty skin. We watched as local airport workers unloaded our plane. To this day, I do not understand why anyone from our government let workers in Kuwait unload our gear. Any other time, the Marine Corps would never miss an opportunity to have a bunch of motivators (Marines) empty an entire plane full of our own gear. While the plane was being unloaded, we stuffed ourselves into a city transit bus and traveled to Camp Victory in northern Kuwait, accompanied by an armed escort of Kuwaiti police. On the bus ride, we all stared out of the window at the bleak early morning desert landscape and watched an absurd Kuwaiti movie. Even though we couldn't understand what they were saying, it was nice to laugh at the terrible quality of the filmmaking.

We arrived at Camp Victory roughly an hour later. I was another step closer to arriving in Iraq. We got off the bus and all walked immediately into a rules-of-engagement briefing, where we watched a movie with a Judge Advocate General officer giving us the many reasons for using lethal force. From there, we went to our tents, where we were to spend the night. The tents looked like a small city of green canvas. Stepping inside mine, I noticed the smell of dirt and wood. The floors were made of wooden pallets covered with plywood. Military folding cots lined the inside of the tent, one row on each side and one down the middle. Excited to see power outlets inside, I immediately pulled out the portable speakers for my CD player and plugged them in. I was about to play some music for the whole tent to enjoy until I realized I had forgotten to plug my European plug adapter into a power converter. The smell of burning electronics filled my nostrils as I realized the next place for my speakers was going to be the trash can. I laid down on my cot and watched the top of the tent flutter from the wind beating it outside.

The next morning, the company gunnery sergeant ("Gunny") handed us our ammunition. Everyone walked up to him to get the ammunition for their rifle. I got a 200-round drum for my M249 SAW and pulled 100 rounds out to put in a cloth magazine pouch that was easier to haul around attached to the weapon. We called this cloth pouch a "nut sack," fittingly. It was bad enough that we had to carry our weapons with us everywhere in Kuwait and Iraq, but we SAW gunners also had the 100-round pouch in our cargo pocket that would rub the outside of our leg raw. We walked around bowlegged like cowboys when we went to the chow hall or the phones to make a call home. That night I called to notify my family I was safe and that I loved them. After I made my calls home, one of the senior Marines in my squad, Corporal Patrick Dunn, told me about midnight chow for the Army folks who stood guard on Camp Victory. We sat in the chow hall and devoured Otis Spunkmeyer muffins and preserved chocolate milk in juice-box-sized containers. It was nice to have Marines who had made this trip before. This was Corporal

Dunn's third combat deployment to Iraq. He was in the initial invasion in 2003 and in Fallujah in 2004. He and I were both very tall and from the same state, which made for simple conversations. Dunn, along with many others, was only supposed to stay with us for 120 days before being sent home. A lot of us called them the "120-dayers."

In my squad alone, besides Dunn, I had Corporal Matt Cannan and Lance Corporal Marty Mortenson, also three-time Iraq combat veterans, "three-pump chumps," making their last trip before they were to get out of the Marine Corps to begin their civilian lives. My squad was tight. We had trained together for five months prior to deploying. However, it was in the field that we learned how each of us thought, how we would react, how we were supposed to move in certain situations. It got to the point where we could look at a silhouette walking in the dark and be able to tell who it was by their gait and the way they carried themselves. My squad leader, Sergeant Gary Laws, was a veteran of Afghanistan. This was his first trip to Iraq as well.

The first time I met him, I couldn't help but smile when he butchered my last name. He had a lisp that made him pronounce my name as "Thores." I was happy I could keep my bearing until he left the room the first time I heard it. He was a good squad leader. He cared a lot about all the Marines in his squad. Many were veterans of Fallujah, that having been their first deployment. Although we all trained in separate teams during our predeployment training on Camp Pendleton, while in Iraq, we ended up being moved around to best fit the needs of the platoon and the squad.

After a few days in Kuwait, many of us younger Marines were itching to go into battle. We loaded our gear onto C-130 airplanes and stood in the chilly early evening air. Like ducks, we followed each other into the loud C-130s via the rear ramp and found a seat in the red webbing that lined the sides of the aircraft. Packed like sardines, we watched as the lights over Kuwait were shut out by the closing ramp door. The engines droned a hypnotic hum as we all sat quietly, collecting our thoughts, a sort of calm before the storm. I had to urinate so badly the entire flight, but I didn't want to get up in front of our Alpha Company commanding officer, Captain Kelsey Thompson, so I anxiously held it. I also never realized there was a head (Navy and Marine jargon for a toilet) on board the C-130, so my options were limited regardless. Before I knew it, we were on our final approach, on what felt like my last flight. We felt like we were spiraling toward the earth as if we had been shot down, but suddenly the plane leveled out and the pilot safely landed us onto the dark, windy airstrip of Al Asad, Iraq.

That first night, I recall writing in the leather-bound journal my sister had gifted me for Christmas prior to my deployment. Arriving at Al Asad while suffering from an upper respiratory illness, I had to ensure I had an ample supply of cough syrup to combat whatever I had caught. I made a trip to the Post Exchange (PX) with a friend and my trusty SAW by my side. I picked up some cough syrup, candy, and miscellaneous hygiene items. We then walked back to our tent. The dry and dusty air robbed the saliva from our mouth, leaving a powdery toothpaste-like grit in its place. After drinking about half a bottle of cough syrup, I was ready for bed. Once again, we stayed in canvas tents, on canvas cots, and fell asleep to the sound of the wind beating against the sides of the tent.

The next afternoon, we loaded into seven-ton trucks and prepared to depart for Ramadi. It felt as though we were on a different planet. Gazing up at the orange overcast sky and never-ending desert, we traveled down a combination of dirt and paved roads. I don't remember saying much of anything the entire ride. No one did. We all looked around, taking in the bleak surroundings. I remember feeling alone, though my brothers surrounded me. The country was so desolate. I tried to predict where the enemy might be hiding. I was trying to pick out the piece of cover I would get down behind if we were to get blown up or get in a firefight. Nothing happened.

As we pulled up to Camp Ramadi, the smell of burning trash polluted the air. A large water tower on the camp was littered with graffiti from units stationed there. So far, everything was quiet, and it didn't feel like a war to me. I was expecting it to be some kind of *Saving Private Ryan* entrance with bullets and explosions surrounding our convoy, but there was silence, eerie silence, as though the enemy were plotting our demise as they watched us enter their city. Fresh game for their hunt.

We unloaded our gear and made the cabin-like huts feel like a home for the week we would be staying there. Each hut (hooch) had four bunks, enough for a part of our squad. Our gear was stowed under the beds and in the common space between them. We were there to acclimatize before we moved to our forward operating base (FOB), Hurricane Point. We had been traveling for a couple of days now; I was tiring of constantly moving locations and gear. I was jet-lagged, tired, and still getting over whatever sickness was hanging on. When we had finished settling in, I was ready for a shower. I walked to the shower trailer carrying my fresh change of clothes, my towel, and my hygiene kit. Lance Corporal Chris Garcia, a Fallujah veteran, and I were the last ones to finish up in the trailer. I opened the shower curtain and found our boots were the only articles left in the trailer. Someone had taken our clothes and towels. Garcia and I laughed as we tried to figure out how we were going to get back to our hooch, which was about fifty meters away. I looked into my boots and noticed my socks were still stuffed inside, so I took one out and slid the elastic band over my penis and tried to tuck my testicles inside the band—all to no avail. I put my boots on and laughed at my reflection in the mirror one last time before I departed for the walk to my hooch. Garcia soon followed behind me in the same manner. I quickly looked outside and saw one of the other Marines from my platoon. He found my boxers lying outside the shower area on the gravel and handed them to me. I replaced the sock with my boxers. As soon as we exited the shower trailer, cameras flashed. I felt like a celebrity as the shutters from a few members of my company clicked away and the sound of disposable cameras winding filled my ears. The members of my company laughed as they yelled for their friends to come out of their hooch. Garcia and I confidently waved and strutted as we walked back over the small pebbles that covered the ground, into the hooch.

We didn't do too much at Camp Ramadi. We had some short classes our squad leaders gave us on our area of operations, but mostly we horsed around. Often, we would wrestle around inside the hooch with everyone cheering on. Some guys, like me, liked to play video games on their computers while listening to music. It helped pass the time and allowed me to forget where I was for a while. We did anything we could think of to pass the time; smoking was something that definitely helped. I was always against smoking until about a month before we left for Iraq. Everyone in my platoon had convinced me I would start in Iraq anyway, so I succumbed to peer pressure and bought a pack of cigarettes. When I first arrived in Iraq, I was smoking about a pack of Marlboro Reds a day. Almost everyone enjoyed smoking. It was a chance to have a break and a talk. Every once in a while, when we'd be outside smoking, we could hear an explosion in the distance. I had my first experience of being mortared when we were at Camp Ramadi, but the mortars landed far away from us, so I wasn't too afraid.

We were soon heading out to our FOB, which was across the Euphrates River from Camp Ramadi. We loaded into the seven-ton trucks and were told this time to keep our heads below the armor. The trucks seemed cobbled together, with steel panels lining the troop compartment and sandbags sandwiched between them. We sat on top of two layers of sandbags which were stained with sweat, spilled Gatorade and Rip-Its, and the butts of cigarettes. The side panels were made secure by finishing the sandwich with ratchet straps. To top it off, the rear doors were just one panel of steel which made for arguments as to who would sit next to the death doors when there was a risk from roadside bombs. It didn't seem that we were fighting for the greatest military in the world, judging by the vehicles we were relying on to transport us into a combat zone.

I was very nervous at that point, my stomach in knots. We were going into the city. From what we could see of it from Camp Ramadi, it looked huge—much larger than I had pictured an Iraqi city. Large three- and five-story residential and commercial buildings were everywhere. It was only about a five-minute ride to our new home at Hurricane Point, where I was based for the rest of the deployment. Learning we could finally drop our gear and make the place home for the next seven months was a relief. After settling in, we attended an orientation brief that familiarized us with the locations on the base. It was much smaller than Camp Ramadi, at the point where the Euphrates River splits off around the city, in its westernmost part. Our barracks had concrete walls and a tin roof. I remember thinking that mortars would travel right through the roof if they hit it. I envisioned how it would look with all of us sleeping; I wondered, "Would it go through the guy sleeping on the top bunk, or would his body absorb the shrapnel and save the Marine on the bottom bunk?" I wasn't eager to find out. Thinking about it left a knot in my stomach for the first few days. I chose my bed and took the top bunk. I figured we were in a bad spot no matter what. When I laid in bed to test the comfort, I noticed my legs were too long for the footer. I also noticed the bars on the footer of the bunk were hollow aluminum. I grabbed the bolt cutters we had to cut locks off buildings when patrolling and cut the decorative support rods off the footer so I could allow my feet to hang off the end. It was much more comfortable.

We had more briefs over the next few days. During this time, all the squad leaders, platoon sergeants, and platoon commanders left to patrol with a platoon from 2/5 to get an idea of what it was like to be out in Ramadi. Everyone came back just fine. They described what the city looked like, and we all listened, with no enemy contact being made. I thought to myself, "Well, they came back just fine, so there must not be too much enemy activity in the area."

What I didn't realize was that, in the early spring, the terrorists didn't fight as hard when the weather didn't cater to their comfort. We continued to train with our weapons and helped to ready the Humvees (HMMWV—high mobility multipurpose wheeled vehicle) that were turned over to us by 2/5. As I looked at every Humvee, I noticed there wasn't one that didn't have damage from either small-arms fire or improvised explosive devices somewhere on them. Even the one with the Red Cross logo on it had bullet holes in it. I also noticed a lot of the armor for them was just thick pieces of rusted steel welded to the vehicle in an unsightly fashion; "farmer armor," we called it. We also had a couple Humvees that didn't have latches for the rear doors. Every time we left for a patrol, we had to search Hurricane Point to find a stick to lie across the brackets so the doors would stay shut and we wouldn't fall out. Sometimes the stick would fail or get lost on patrol, and we would have to hold the doors shut manually while driving around Ramadi. We were fortunate the enemy didn't want to fight right away when we arrived. It was as though they had allowed us time to figure out some of the city and settle ourselves in. It was foolish of them and potentially detrimental to us. We got complacent. We were comfortable with the somewhat quiet month that March proved to be.

On top of adjusting to the new routine, our command thought it would be a great idea to implement something they coined "morale suppression." Their idea, to my understanding, was to keep our morale low for the first month and then boost it later on by having simple amenities. For the first 30 days after our arrival at Hurricane Point, we could not listen to music or use our personal laptops to watch movies or play games, and they removed the televisions 2/5 had left for us in our hooch. For entertainment, we could only read. I don't recall there being a library or an excellent selection of books available, so that option didn't help either. Our gunnery sergeant would come around and periodically check the company's living quarters for people disobeying orders, confiscating laptops and MP3 players from anyone caught using them. I hated that order; it made no sense to me. There we were, putting our lives on the line and they wanted to take away simple things we'd grown accustomed to having to help us relax and not be on edge. The situation made for a lot of bitter Marines and a lot of talk of how we could get back at command. Adding to the frustrations, concerns about hygiene led to the burning of the old mattresses 2/5 had left for us at the Government Center, the administrative offices of Anbar Province we pulled regular post duty at. I would have preferred to sleep on a dirty mattress instead of a cot, which I didn't fit on anyway because of my height. At least we could keep the mattresses at Hurricane Point for the deployment. Gunny even found it necessary to remove the shower curtains back at our FOB, for reasons that still remain a mystery. The Government Center didn't have working plumbing, so we didn't have access to showers there. We only had the showers back at Hurricane Point; we would bathe with baby wipes at the Government Center. The water supply at Hurricane Point was limited, so when "personnel other than grunts" (POGs) would take long showers while we were out on patrol or at the Government Center, we'd return to no water for the showers. At best we only had cold water because POGs had taken their time in the showers.

For restrooms, we had the standard portable toilets at Hurricane Point, the kind commonly found at construction sites in the United States. The ones we had always seemed to be filled to the brim with excrement; if they weren't, we would get the blue "monster" splash as our shit fell into the empty tank. Also, this gathering place always made for interesting times if you ventured to the porta-shitter at night. Inevitably, you would hear the turning of magazine pages in the porta-shitter next to you, followed by the sound of someone masturbating. Then there were the die-hard guys who would bring their laptop into the sauna-like loo, making for a colorful display inside their porta-shitter against the black of the night surrounding it. I, too, succumbed to this guilty pleasure. All cares go out the window when death is constantly knocking at your door and privacy is nonexistent.

CHAPTER 2

Ramadi

Complacency Kills

March was a fairly quiet month. One of our first patrols was in the extensive market area of Ramadi, also known as the souk, in the evening. A combat photographer was attached to our platoon to document our patrol, which lasted a few hours. It was my first time walking through a marketplace in another country. The souk seemed so primitive and foreign. Animal carcasses hung from hooks, skinned but with hoofs or paws (of what appeared to have been dogs) still fully intact. Fish with green slime and littered with flies sat on open wooden trays alongside vegetables and fruit. Old men did their best to keep the flies off the exposed meat by fanning it with paper or brush-like whips made of animal hair. It was a far cry from where I was used to getting my groceries back home in my small town.

I turned the corner for an alley and heard a whooshing sound, almost like a garden hose running, and saw a cow with its throat cut. The blood was pouring into the middle of the street. We had to walk through it. It mixed with the other waste that ran through the street, creating a black sludge that smelled of rot, excrement, and blood. The cow lay on its side and slightly kicked as it bled to death, wide-eyed and looking at the butcher who stood staring at our patrol, the bloody knife on the table next to him—my first experience with the process of halal meat.

During these first patrols, the Marines in my platoon noticed one issue with our lieutenant (LT). He was also on his first deployment. He was very kind, kept himself in shape, rarely cussed, and was very knowledgeable about military tactics and the culture of Iraq. He was a graduate of an Ivy League university. I believe he truly felt, at first, that we could make a difference for the residents of Ramadi. Hell, we all did. The only issue we found with him was that he was left-handed. This usually doesn't pose a problem, although the spent rounds fired from his rifle ejected into his face. The biggest issue, however, is the location of the magazine release on the M4 service rifle he carried. It is on the right side of the weapon and, given he held the weapon slung across his body to use his left shoulder, always bumped his body armor and the gear attached to it. We'd be patrolling and would hear the magazine fall out and slam onto the road. When this first began, he'd quickly bend down and pick it up, hoping no one saw. We did. In fact, we counted every time we heard the magazine fall. He would get so frustrated. We'd be quietly patrolling the streets when you'd hear "Whack!" as the magazine hit the ground. "Fuck!" would then accompany a figure bent down in the street trying to remain tactical while retrieving his magazine.

Running always made the issue worse. I remember a few times we'd hear the magazine drop and watch as the interpreter would stop, pick up the magazine, and run it back up to the LT, who'd be shaking his head and mumbling, "Fucking magazine." Or we would witness his attempt to dash across the street during a firefight. As the magazine would fall, he'd kick it in the direction of where he was moving, where he'd pick it up. This alone provided us with entertainment in some scary situations and, unfortunately for him, led to the rest of us having comedic relief. I think we ended up counting upwards of thirty times the magazine had fallen out of his rifle by the end of the deployment. The Iraqi civilians would enjoy watching the spectacle as well. I like to think it showed them we were human behind the body armor, sunglasses, and weapons.

The Iraqis in the marketplace didn't seem to mind us while we patrolled through their places of business and patronage. Some of them would wave and some would blankly stare, or "mad dog" us as we called it. The marketplace was also a great tell to see what type of day we were going to have on patrol. If it was busy, we were less likely to be attacked that day; if it was vacant, we'd better be ready for an ambush. The civilians usually knew if the mujahideen were in their area. When we'd arrive, the civilians would close shop because they knew the enemy was about to attack us. Closing up shop was typically more obvious than just locking a door. The shops had garage-door-like anti-theft bars or panels that came down in front of the shop. The owners would pull the gates down and leave the area, making a racket in the process. They also knew we weren't afraid to use our weapons, both on patrol and while at the Government Center.

As a part of our patrolling and post rotation, we would go out to the Government Center in the center of the city, which contained the governmental offices for Anbar Province, and stand post. We stood post for six hours and then took a break for six hours while a different platoon took over. While on break, we'd get a workout in, eat, watch movies, fill sandbags for posts, or try to get some sleep. The many improvements the Government Center needed were made while the platoons were off post. Working parties of Marines, typically junior ones, did these improvements. Given how active the Government Center was, we usually only averaged four hours of sleep per night. We stayed there for four days and then moved back to Hurricane Point to patrol the streets of Ramadi for four days. Some days we'd have a few hours to rest between patrols and would sleep in the common space of the Government Center. It took a couple of weeks to get used to the odd hours, but it became a part of my biological clock and daily routine, which made it easier. In the beginning, we were going out on three or four patrols a day, which made for an exhausting four days; we looked forward to going to the Government Center to stand post and rest.

Poppin' Cherries

It amazed me how little combat we experienced in those first weeks. We had done our share of post at the Government Center, but no insurgents had attacked during those times. Overall, the other companies in the battalion were experiencing the same thing. The first time our platoon saw any combat was because of my squad's actions.

We went out and set an ambush, where we tried to catch the enemy, unprepared, setting up to attack us near the Government Center. We would set these ambushes at night to mask our movements. My squad was in a small bank just to the south of the Government Center. It was so cold outside that night; I didn't realize it got so cold in the desert. My friend Lance Corporal Marty Mortenson, a veteran of the initial invasion and Fallujah, and I were on top of the bank. We were lying right next to each other, shivering as we scanned the area for any movement. We were up there for around an hour when we got word an Army convoy was going to be traveling down the main road, Route Michigan, through the city within a few minutes. As the convoy approached our position, an improvised explosive device (IED) exploded on Route Michigan. It startled Mortenson and me, shaking us out of our frozen state. I began searching near the plume of smoke for movement. Mortenson saw movement on top of a building about 250 meters away from our position and called it out. At that time during the deployment, a citywide curfew was in place; no one was supposed to be outside of their home past ten o'clock. Mortenson called in over the radio that he saw movement on a roof to our east as he prepared an illumination round for his M203 grenade launcher. We were cleared to engage any threats. I had set my M249 SAW (Squad Automatic Weapon) on the edge of the roof; I readied my sights on the guy, waiting for Mortenson to fire the illumination round. Knowing I had Mortenson, now a three-tour Iraq veteran, alongside me, I knew we would be okay. I had stopped shivering; I was warm. I patiently sat behind my SAW while my breathing became slow and deep as I did my best to keep my sights on the tiny figure 250 meters out.

Mortenson fired the illumination round perfectly above the building of the silhouetted person. I waited for the round to pop and cut through the darkness. When it finally did, it was as though the sun had ripped through the night sky. The figure moved back and forth, as though he was wondering what was happening, looking out into the darkness, trying to find us. I fired a burst from my SAW and watched the tracers impact around the figure a short second later. Mortenson immediately began firing at the figure, who was now moving toward a door on the rooftop. I let out another long burst from my SAW, pointing it right where the enemy was running; into the door and into our barrage of bullets. It was quiet for a second as we both stopped firing. During that pause, a burst of full-auto AK rifle fire pumped rounds in our direction.

The rounds went over our heads, having come from the door the figure had darted into. We opened fire again and watched our bullets rip into the building and the door. It was my first firefight. As the veterans of Operation *Iraqi Freedom*'s first deployment (OIF 1) and OIF 2 said, my cherry was popped. Though the firefight was short, I was drunk with excitement. Mortenson and I looked at each other. He was looking at me with his ear-to-ear grin that he always had and asked, "Well, whatcha think? Fucking cool, huh?" I had a huge smile and, with a dry mouth, replied something like, "Fucking awesome."

I was eager to do an assessment of the individual we had just engaged. I pictured myself walking to the top of the building and finding a dead terrorist, envisioning how great that would have felt. As our platoon gathered on the road to head out to the building, one of our guys had a negligent discharge with his weapon, narrowly missing another Marine. The LT was so upset because of the Marine's mistake that he made us return to the forward operating base (FOB) without going to check out the building. I was pretty disappointed, but I suppose everything happens for a reason. Besides, it's not like it was the last time we'd have the opportunity to do our job as infantry Marines. Given it was the second time this Marine had had a negligent discharge, the platoon treated him like an outcast for a few weeks. Although I didn't hold any grudges against him, I kept my distance. I avoided him until he was writing a letter home one day and asked me how to spell "lonely." I figured Iraq was the last place anyone should feel that way, so I forgave him and gave him the correct spelling.

Around the end of March, things really began to pick up. Terrorists were coming out of their hibernation, hungry for our infidel blood. We had our first firefight as a full platoon when we were in the westernmost part of the marketplace in the city center of Ramadi. We were driving through the streets on our way back to the FOB when rounds began impacting the sides of our vehicles and cracking over our heads.

"Contact!" someone called out, but we did not know where it was coming from. Chaos reigned. Nothing we could have done up to that time would have trained us to deal with the total confusion of being shot at in a large city, especially with civilians running around just as confused as we were. Our vehicles pushed through the kill zone of the ambush, and the patrol got stuck in the middle of the souk. Immediately, Corporal Matt Cannan called for all of us to dismount our high-back Humvee. Some of our squad went out the back, but there wasn't much room for all to exit quickly in the same direction. Those of us in the front jumped over the top and onto the cab, where the driver and assistant driver sat, awkwardly stepped onto the hood, and finally onto the ground. Our gear seemed to want to keep our body's momentum going into the ground and we stumbled to catch our footing alongside the trash that littered the streets. We immediately sought cover along the shops nearest us as bullets still skipped and snapped around the area. Sergeant Laws decided we should run down a street to move toward the enemy. As we moved, it was determined we were not going in the right direction. We sprinted down the street a couple of blocks and then had to return the way we had just come.

Almost everyone mumbled "fuck" as we U-turned around without slowing our run and ran back toward the convoy. While turning around, we could see a six-story building near the vehicles. Sergeant Laws decided we would move into that building and get to the top for a better vantage point. My team was in the lead, so we began our climb on the one staircase in the building. I believe Lance Corporal Chris Garcia took point up the stairs, followed by another squad member and then Cannan. I followed Cannan while Lance Corporal Kenny Morgan was behind me. We started running up the stairs; by the fifth floor we were at a walk. Upon entering every floor of the building, one person held security on the stairs as the rest of us cleared out that level. Some rooms had terrified civilians in them, but a majority of them were vacant. As we neared the top, I remember Cannan laughing and saying, "Of course we picked the tallest building!"

We finally made it to the top, gasping for air and trying to keep our heads about us. Morgan and I went to the right once we were on the roof of the building. The radio, with a ten-foot whip antenna attached to it, was carried by Morgan, who usually folded it down to be about three feet above his daypack. The antenna was constructed similar to tent poles, allowing for quick unfolding and folding. If we were deeper in the city, we needed the full ten feet to ensure clear communications with our battalion command post. Morgan and I both took a knee and looked down into the city. Just as we kneeled down, a bullet impacted the wall directly behind us. We got down, smiled with relief at each other that the bullet had missed, and made it known to all around us where the fire was coming from. I crawled farther away from Morgan, and he did the same. We popped up again and searched the area. I saw a guy in white casually walking around as small-arms fire around the city drowned out any other sounds. The fact that he walked around so casually in a firefight made him suspicious enough for me, even though I couldn't see exactly what he was carrying. I placed my sights on him and followed him as he walked. He disappeared under the cloth overhang of a storefront, so I let a burst go where I thought he was walking. I wondered if I had hit him. I never saw him after that. Rounds were still coming at us from all directions. A call came over the radio from our platoon sergeant, Staff Sergeant Daniel "Papi" Santiago, to load back up into the vehicles because we were going to a mosque where one of our Marines had seen military age males run into.

Descending the staircase was much easier, and we immediately returned to our high-back Humvee. We sped around the souk and arrived at the mosque a short time later. My truck was the first to dismount. Our battalion headquarters had cleared us to search the mosque prior to our arrival, so once we were out of our vehicle, we crashed through the metal gates. We hurried through the compound; I took security along the outside of one of the buildings. As soon as I knew another Marine was with me, I took off toward the next building with my weapon up, ready to fire. I entered a courtyard and noticed three men in their forties across the courtyard. My blood surged through my body as I yelled at them to get down and pointed my weapon at them. They stood in disbelief, glaring at me in a way that made me aware they felt we weren't supposed to be in the mosque. I kept moving toward them and yelling while Papi moved to my left and helped me to keep them from overtaking me. They stood still and stared at me. As we moved up to them, I screamed for them to get down as I pointed at the ground. Papi was also yelling at them. They moved slowly, so I helped one of them to the ground by forcing his head; with that demonstration, the others quickly got down on their faces. Papi told the interpreter to make sure the men in front of us knew to keep their heads down and not to look around. As they lay there, they kept looking around. I asked the interpreter if the men had understood him, and the interpreter confirmed they knew what he was saying. I forced the man's head to the ground. Once again, the others next to him complied with our commands. After we had zip-tied their hands and blindfolded them, we brought them into the main part of the mosque where my platoon guide, Sergeant Erik Sphoon, was located. We had been told to bring all personnel under control (PUC) to this central area.

Once inside the mosque, I realized why the men we had zip-tied wouldn't listen to our commands. Our platoon found several AK-47 rifles, ammunition, and a pair of night-vision goggles (NVGs). Once we had confirmed there were weapons and told the PUCs what we had found, they talked. Some of them admitted to using the weapons, others wouldn't say a word. We loaded them into the back of our high-back Humvee. Since the Humvee was already crowded with Marines, we set them all cross-legged on the floor at our feet.

That was the first time I had an actual terrorist sitting in front of me, alive. I wanted to kill him so badly; I'm sure he wanted to do the same to me. We had them zip-tied and blindfolded with either a sandbag or empty box. The one in front of me kept struggling to stand so, to make sure he wouldn't try to get away from us, I put my foot on his testicles and applied pressure. I could have sworn I felt one testicle pop under the pressure of my foot. He cried the entire way back to the FOB, but he also never tried to get up like a couple of the other PUCs. After that day's events, I found myself slipping into the darkness of combat. The extreme highs of surviving being hunted, paired with the anger as the people who were trying to kill you sit beside you. Sweating on you. Crying by you. I often wondered what they would do to me in a similar scenario, with me as the captive. There were plenty of videos available online at that point of captive men in orange jumpsuits to give me somewhat of an answer to what my demise would be.

Many of our patrols out on the town were uneventful. We handed out candy or food to kids and searched house-to-house for weapons, going block-to-block. We met a lot of interesting civilians there. I once ran into a woman who had crucifixes all over her house with photos of Jesus. When we entered her house, she said, "Christian," pointing to herself and smiling. "Christian."

I didn't care either way that she was Christian, so long as she didn't want to blow me up or shoot me. She also said her daughter was living in Detroit and was going to school there. We always enjoyed talking with the locals when they were welcoming. We had run into women our age who spoke perfect English, who traveled to America and went to college in the States. One wanted to move back to Iraq because she missed her family. It's unbelievable how small the world is. The Iraqi people who seemed happy we were there were always very kind and accommodating. "Chai?" they would ask, offering us tea. Some were more than happy we were keeping insurgents out of their neighborhood. The chai prepared for us was very good; I sure miss it. I don't know if it actually tasted great or if the situations we found ourselves in made it taste all the better. It felt human and helped to bring light to us, if even for a moment. It always made me feel good to know some people appreciated what we were doing, even as I doubted our reasons for being there.

When we established an ambush position for an evening, we would round up the family from the house we were taking over and make everyone sit in the same room. We took this measure for our safety as well as theirs. We would always have Marines in the room with them to monitor them. I always enjoyed coming back into the house, while set up in an ambush, to hang out with the locals because a lot of them were just as interested in us as we were in them. It was fun to interact, even though we were putting them out for the evening, and not by their choice. Once, when we were keeping guard on a family, they watched TV, a music channel similar to MTV except Middle Eastern. They played a track of one of their Middle Eastern artists and then followed it up with a Green Day music video. It was a weird experience for me to see them watching a music video from our culture. I didn't think they liked anything from our Western world. Another one of their videos came on and one kid from the family got up and began dancing, so I joined him by doing the best dance I could do while carrying my weapon and with all my gear on. I felt as though I could have been in the Broadway show *River Dance* as we all laughed at my expense. It was such a wonderful experience for all of us to mingle with the locals, more than just shaking their hands but actually interacting for periods of time. Seeing the happiness and trust in someone's eyes as we entered their house was such a welcoming feeling, knowing we had gained their trust prior. It made everything seem more human, almost neighborly. It seemed, though, that situations always came along to dampen the appreciation I had gained for the local populace.

We were on a patrol in the southern part of our area of operations, conducting our house-to-house searches. Our squad had come upon a house that was shot up and burned. We all entered it and were assessing the damage. Except for the blackened and burned debris all over the floor, nothing was really left. No one could have been living there recently. But, suddenly, we heard a noise. It came from down the hallway. My guts tightened and I felt weak. We were caught off guard. I turned around, along with everyone else, and we froze, mouths agape and heads tilted slightly forward, like prey startled by a predator. We waited for the sound to come again. No one moved a muscle. Our eyes darted back and forth between each other. We heard a faint moan from the stairwell that led to the roof. We walked down the hallway. The LT, Corporal Patrick Dunn, Marty Mortenson, and I walked down the burned and debris-ridden hallway. We were trying to be as quiet as possible. Dunn was the first to the stairwell. I watched as he slowly pied off the stairs with his weapon, rounding the corner to the stairwell with his weapon up, ready to fire. As he fully exposed himself to the stairwell, he lowered his muzzle and laughed.

"It's a girl," he said. She moaned a haunting sound again when she saw Dunn.

Loud, drawn-out moans poured from the girl's mouth, almost like a wounded animal.

"Shores, get up there." Dunn said, smiling and gesturing with his rifle for me to take point up the stairs.

Remnants of a broken bed frame lay on the stairs, a perfect obstacle to put in the middle of a staircase. I walked past the LT and Mortenson and looked at Dunn.

"Why me? I have a fucking SAW," I said.

"Because you're the tallest and you're a boot," Dunn, just about as tall as me, said with a grin. A "boot" is a new Marine on their first deployment. I didn't argue any further because I knew my place.

I cautiously walked up the stairs, my SAW on my hip, pointing toward this moaning girl. As I got closer, I noticed she had a full, dark, splotchy goatee. Her attire was made up of a pink nightgown adorned with a fruit pattern, and she was barefoot. She smelled terrible and was filthy. I extended my gloved hand to keep her at bay after she gestured toward me. She moaned and stared at me as I slowly moved around her to the roof door at the top of the stairs. I noticed she had something in a pan on the stairs,

"Naan and curdled milk are mixed in a fucking pan," I shouted down to the guys at the bottom of the stairs.

I reached the roof by myself. Dunn had been making his way up behind me. We cleared the roof and the rest of the house, finding nothing of importance. We stayed there as the LT tried to figure out what this girl was doing. Someone found a neighbor, and we connected our interpreter with them. Soon an old woman appeared at the entrance to the house. She lived in a house attached to the back of the destroyed house we were in. It turned out the young girl was this old woman's daughter. The mother had locked the poor, young teenage girl in the burned-out house because she didn't want to care for her disabled child. Or maybe she didn't have the means to care for her. Either way, it was a sad situation. They treated the teenager as if she were a feral dog. We all had some choice words for the woman as we walked past her, knowing she would continue to mistreat this girl. I felt so bad that someone could just cast aside their own blood to live like an animal. I had never before seen anything like that and never wanted to again. It broke my heart to leave that house, knowing the young girl would be kept there. Knowing they had no social services to report to, I hated to think what that girl's future would bring.

April

Before I knew it, April was upon us. We had been in the country for a month and nothing too terrible had happened. This specific day, I was hungry and looking forward to getting off the radio watch in our command center at the FOB. As I walked back toward my barracks, my eyes locking on to the door of the mess hall, I felt a massive explosion, the largest I had felt yet. At the distance I was from the explosion, I felt the odd shock-wave disruption just before the noise filled my ears. Looking out into the city and seeing an enormous mushroom cloud, I immediately ran back into the command center to see what was going on. A suicide bomber had blown up an outpost Bravo Company was operating out of, two blocks from the Government Center. They immediately directed our platoon on quick-reaction force to get on our vehicles and stage, preparing to leave and assist Bravo Company. Roughly ten minutes later, our LT came running from the command center and jumped into his Humvee. We started moving out. No one really knew what was going on. We knew a suicide bombing had happened and we were going to secure the area. Only team leaders had mobile radios, so we relied on trying to listen in on what was going on through the vehicle's radio. I was in a turreted Humvee, with my SAW as the gun mounted on top of the vehicle.

We left the safety of our FOB and sped down the road toward the smoke. When we arrived, we could see debris strewn across the intersection. It was just off Route Michigan, at what we called Intersection 295. We pulled up into our position near the bent frame of the bomber's vehicle. When we stopped, I immediately checked the area around our Humvee for secondary IEDs, as we always did. What I saw took a moment to sink in: four fingers and part of the hand of the suicide bomber were lying on the sidewalk. The image resembled carne asada but with fingers poking out of it. Small pieces of other flesh also lay all over, but nothing as identifiable as the four fingers. We stayed there well into the night providing security so Bravo Company could leave the outpost after they destroyed it. The target building was destroyed by the bomber, but no Marines were killed. Only a few suffered injuries from being blown from their beds, dislocating shoulders and experiencing concussions. It was unbelievable to witness that explosion and see that no Marines were killed.

A few nights later, a suicide bomber drove a station wagon into an Army Bradley fighting vehicle, knocking the tracks off its right side. We had to go out and help provide security again for the bomb site. The debris needed to be cleaned up and the Bradley needed to be towed from the area. As we pulled up, I couldn't see much of what was going on. With my NVGs, I could see that one body had been blown across the street, but I couldn't see anything else. When we drove by on our way out, I got a better view of the bomber and his vehicle as there were Marines and soldiers using their flashlights to illuminate the scene. The vehicle was a mangled mess in the front and the rear had been on fire. Behind the back tire, the bomber was in the fetal position, burned to a crisp. Another man had been blown across the road. I'm not sure if he was a part of the attack or just a bystander, either way, his body was destroyed. Severe injuries had turned his legs and arms into tattered and smashed flesh. Blood streaks led up to where he lay dead, mouth and eyes open, staring into the nothingness of Ramadi. We all laughed as we drove by. In the darkness, we could also see that the bomber's buttocks were still on fire and joked about his rear end being on fire. "Serves him right for being a terrorist," I thought.

Bodies

Being back at Hurricane Point felt like being back home, where our beds were, where the hot chow was, where the internet and phones were. It was also where a certain corporal, the company's working-party aficionado, worked hard. Our company gunnery sergeant ("Gunny") would tell the corporal what needed to be done for the day, and he would go around to the two platoons who were back from patrols resting to make a request:

"Two bodies. I need two bodies."

We all hated that he asked for "bodies." He was from another platoon. Demanding that two of our bodies assist him with the day's duties was something we hated when he came around. We always told him, "We're Marines, Corporal, not bodies. We're still alive."

Not seeming to care, he'd always reply, "You know what I mean. Now give me a hand."

That he didn't understand what we were trying to say pissed us off the most. He didn't understand a body is not a Marine. Marines are Marines. He got a kick out of frustrating us when his silhouette would appear through the doorway of our hooch, the sun blinding us in the darkened room.

"Two bodies. Meet me outside. Two bodies." He would speak his words in a callous way, holding up two fingers, and walking around the hooch, looking for us newer guys.

"Fuck you, go get guys from your platoon," we'd reply from the safety of the darkness while lying in our bunks.

He'd seem to find us right when we got back from a patrol or when we were getting to the climax of the movie we were watching. I'd pretend I didn't see him if I was watching a movie with my headphones on. While watching a movie, I would stare at the computer screen, desperately wishing my headphones were embedded in my head so he couldn't physically remove them just to ensure I had heard him.

"Two bodies, Shores, grab a friend," he'd say if he reached me without having snatched someone else up.

His smile expressed a sense of enjoyment while we'd sigh with the realization that it was our turn. I wouldn't have had so much resentment toward the man if he would have just asked for some Marines, but he made a point of asking for two bodies. Making the shift rounds with his platoon, he would stay out at the Government Center. He traveled out there with them until a sniper round hit him, sending him home. He survived, and the saying "Two bodies" never interrupted another movie. It's unfortunate he was a casualty, but I'm also glad I never saw him again.

Boogeymen

Many times, we were out in the city looking for this mystical guy by the name of Zarqawi, a high value target (HVT). We younger Marines never really knew who he was. All we knew was he would have some security surrounding him. In fact, we were often out doing patrols or other missions that were attempts to locate him or associates, unbeknownst to us. We junior Marines never really knew what we were doing and looked to our seniors for any directions as they had both the experience and the communications gear. Our battle-weary senior lance corporals and corporals would tell us to just keep an eye out for anything weird and shoot anyone who looked bad. Had we known Zarqawi was the mastermind behind the al-Tawhid wal-Jihad organization and a prominent leader in al-Qaeda, we probably would have taken everything a little more seriously.

Some nights, we'd have to escort or insert SEAL teams, or FBI or CIA personnel. One night, we took a wrong turn while inserting a SEAL team and an IED blew us up. The Humvee carrying the SEALs was right in front of the seven-ton I was in; the IED exploded between our two vehicles. We were only going around twenty miles per hour when the IED when off, so the result could have been disastrous. Thankfully, there were no casualties. We dropped off the SEAL team and proceeded with our mission of moving house-to-house to search for weapons or other pieces of information that could be helpful to coalition forces. A couple of hours later, we were called to pick up the SEAL team again. Apparently, one SEAL had somehow broken his leg and we had to evacuate him. I can't validate if this happened as I wasn't in the evac vehicle. I was busy busting in doors and looking for weapons that didn't seem to exist. We only found lots of babies and scared women living in the cluttered houses that night. On top of all of the confusion, we had to be careful not to step on babies lying on the floor in the dark; I almost did.

We had taken a few people who seemed suspicious as PUC and put them in the back of our high-back Humvees. One of the Marines I was with was tired of lugging around his M16 and shotgun, so he tossed the shotgun in the back of his Humvee. He dropped it over the back of the steel plating as we ran past and we both heard a wail from someone in pain. We stopped and looked at each other; I walked to the back of the Humvee to open the doors. I saw an Iraqi that had been PUC'd by another Marine and put into the vehicle. He had a gash on his forehead from where the shotgun had landed. The other Marine came to the back and saw the Iraqi's head. "Oops," he said. We both laughed. Then he grabbed the shotgun out of the back and I closed the doors. He thought carrying the shotgun was a better idea than leaving it with a guy who we had just taken from his house after being roughed up, zip-tied, blindfolded, and put in the back of a loud vehicle. Apparently, one of the PUCs from that evening was an HVT, one of the top ten most wanted in Iraq at the time.

When we returned from the raid in the morning as the sun was coming up, we dropped off the SEALs at the weapons-clearing barrels and watched as they walked to their waiting helicopter on Hurricane Point. They disappeared into the rising sun on their helo as we stumbled into our hooch.

We would go on many searches throughout the nights and look for Zarqawi door-to-door. It got to the point where we'd get bored waking people up in their homes, so we'd play around with them. We'd make bets on who could sneak in on people and scare them awake. Again, our immaturity showed through.

Our objective was to quietly open the gate to the courtyard, ensuring no one was disturbed. We'd tiptoe up to the front door and make sure it was unlocked, using slow and steady pressure with a synced movement of the latch or knob. Our NVGs would be down as we'd make entry into the dark, eerie abyss of some family's home. I didn't have helmet-mounted NVGs, so I would always stare forward to use my peripheral vision to watch for movement. We would quietly wait and make sure no one was awake. Mouths hanging open and our breath shallow, we prowled around their dark house, searching for the place where they were sleeping. Like the boogeyman, we'd find their bedroom and watch them sleep, only for a moment, to appreciate how quiet we truly were. We were the monsters under their bed, the goblins in their closet, the demons of their dreams.

With the excitement of our quiet successes bursting out of our bodies, we'd start shouting, flashing lights on and off, and pounding or jumping on their bed. We would always laugh at the terrified people. The more scared they were, the funnier it was for us. The sad thing is, I don't know what we would have done if one of the civilians had attacked us out of fear. We probably would have killed them. Thank God that never happened. We were 19-year-olds, acting our age. It was a shameful sight.

Leave it to karma to teach young men. Iraq is where I began to appreciate the principle. When it was my turn to scare someone, I learned of the power of karma. I was so excited because we made entry into the unsuspecting people's home, quiet as ever. We had finished searching the first floor of their home and were moving up the stairs to the second floor. I went left at the top of the stairs and found their bedroom right away. I peeked my head in their room and found both the husband and wife sleeping in their bed. "So far, so good," I thought. I motioned back to the Marines who were down the hallway, instructing them to line up behind me and enter a room quickly. Like a ghoul creeping up to a bed, I stepped up into their bedroom, probably with a huge, stupid grin on my face, and hunkered down. I looked to the door and saw my friends entering the room, too. We were on the verge of being fully prepared. I stood erect, to allow for the most terrifying and authoritative demeanor I could posture, but something stopped me. A rhythmic tapping on my helmet, then one large hit. It felt like it had almost snapped my neck. The ceiling was much shorter than I had expected, and the metal fan blades had their way with my helmet. Of course, the people woke up scared, but not terrified. They found it amusing as we gestured to them what had happened—that their ceiling fan attacked me. We waved to them and told them to sleep well, and we moved on with our never-ending mission to search for Zarqawi, whom we never found.

On one of our day missions to locate one of the many terrorists, we somehow ended up down a stretch of road nicknamed "IED Alley." My squad was dismounted from the vehicles and our lead vehicle accidentally made a wrong turn. We ended up down a road laden with IEDs in our northern area of operations. The decision was made that the only way to get back to a safe area was to run down the street in order to have better dispersion. That's exactly what we did. We ran for our lives. I passed a bunch of my squad members. The LT's radio operator, Corporal Mark Albert, carried the radio and his gear, weighing him down. He was a good friend of mine and was a mentor when I first arrived at Alpha 1/5. He was a seasoned Fallujah veteran as well.

I remember passing him and him saying to me, "Fuck this. This is bullshit. We're gonna get fucking blown up. Fuck this." I looked at him and kept on running. Some guys were carrying the bolt cutters, halligan tools, and sledgehammers. Another Marine and I offered to take some tools from other guys, but they were intent on holding on to them. So we just kept running. It was almost a mile run. I don't know how we made it without being blown up or shot at, but we did.

Not only were there enemy combatants after us, but the city itself had a taste for American blood. A corpsman from our company had to be sent home because he accidentally stuck his hand into a metal fan blade and really cut it up. Ramadi was also a place of low-hanging electrical wires strewn about busy market areas and black sewage lining the streets. Had it been dimly lit and set against eerie music, one could mistake it for a set of a dystopic end-of-the-world movie. If the terrorists would not get me, the wires or the water were next in line.

Many times, our seven-ton trucks plowed through low-hanging wires, as we Marines sat terrified in the back, fearing we were going to be electrocuted. The wires would frequently wrap around the barrel of our machine guns, pulling them from the mount on top of the seven-ton. We would have to stop the patrol and back up to either disentangle the weapon from the web of wires or dismount to recover the weapon now lying in the street.

We knew to keep our heads below the armor in the back of those trucks because we had lined the inside of the bed with sandbags to protect us from IEDs. But it was also nice to lie down in the back so we could watch the wires above. As the seven-ton would break through the wires, we would watch for the "whips," the ones that would stay suspended in the air, whipping about, because of the speed of the truck. They would move in the air like a serpent until they attacked, cracking down at us in the back and causing a moment of panic at the possibility of being wrapped up in them. Once, the wires entangled a Marine in our squad. They whipped across his eye protection and wrapped around his helmet. A moment of sheer terror ensued until another Marine quickly cut the wire with his wire cutters. We all watched as the wire tightened and the Marine grew more uneasy. We attempted to get the attention of the driver and gunner to stop the truck, but the noise of the city and the truck made it impossible for them to hear us. That Marine with the wire cutters was always on top of things and the other is alive because of it.

The souk water, a black, oil-like sewage that filled the roadsides, posed a significant threat to both us and the locals. It surfaced during the night because the sewers had been destroyed by the insurgents a long time before we arrived in the city. By midday, the sludge would almost be gone, but the stench was always there. In the mornings, we had to drive through it; if the gunners weren't paying attention to where the vehicle was headed, they would get splashed with the sludge. The speed of our Humvees combined with the depth of the sewage puddles caused the sludge to splash up and over the whole vehicle and into the machine-gunner's port. This happened to me one morning, while the Judge Advocate General (JAG) officer was riding along in my Humvee. It splashed in my mouth when I looked down to answer a question. I reflexively spit on the JAG officer, but he didn't seem to care. He was more concerned I wash my mouth out with his water than with the fact I had just spit in his face. He was laughing yet concerned. So was I. Nothing like starting the patrol with an unpleasant taste in your mouth. I never got sick, so I'll just chalk up that experience to having an iron stomach.

The local civilians weren't safe from the sewage either. Splashing locals with the sewage water was an unfortunate game we'd play while driving down the narrow streets of the market area of Ramadi. We'd keep an eye out for the best-dressed, cleanest civilian, and we'd ruin their day. Acceleration was the key to getting an enormous wave, and I saw some poor civilians get drenched from head to toe. We'd laugh hysterically and continue driving, watching the poor people stand baffled in the street, soaking in the sewage water from a city that had betrayed their health and safety. I often reflect and shudder, realizing this is exactly what happens when we send teenagers to fight a man's war. For the citizens of Ramadi, we added insult to injury. I'm ashamed to have taken part in such ridiculous acts. We won the hearts and minds of the citizens of Ramadi, for the terrorist's side, with these childish games.

Chicken

After patrolling the same streets week after week, we could pick up on the normal routines of the area and would notice when things were out of the ordinary. It was these minor changes in the daily routines that made the hair on the back of our necks stand up. Not every day was a bad day on patrol. Not every time were we able to sense an ambush but, most of the time, the local populace would unknowingly give the enemy ambush away. On the days when the market was busy and people were out comfortably shopping, we would stray from our patrol as combatants, if only for a moment. We felt comfortable and looked at the unique items for sale in the shops and kiosks. If we saw something we liked, we bought from the vendors, just as the locals did.

The smells of the fresh food always overcame the overflowing sewage smells that typically flooded our senses. Our mouths would water as soon as the smells of the rotisserie chicken, available for purchase from a small kiosk, filled our nostrils. Alongside, a plate full of fresh naan flat bread accompanied the delectable meal. We would hand the kiosk vendor five dollars and he would excitedly hand the juicy rotisserie chicken to us, which was stuffed into another Marine's camelback pouch. Another took the bread from the vendor. We graciously thanked the man for the food and exchanged smiles. We'd then run to our Humvee and throw the food into one of the empty seats.

"Don't eat it yet!" we'd tell the driver and gunner. What a thing to ask as the aroma of fresh food filled the vehicle. Anything was better than an MRE (meal, ready to eat) or the highly processed chow-hall food. We were quickly back on our patrol after dropping off the food, looking for any threats to our lives or anything out of the ordinary.

When it was time to move to another area of town, all five of us in the Humvee enjoyed a warm, juicy chicken lunch with the best naan I've ever tasted. We ate the chicken down to the bone in a matter of seconds. Like vultures, we left no meat behind on the carcass. I was never too afraid of being poisoned when we unexpectedly bought food from vendors in the market. If they were going to poison us, it was, to me, worth the risk of the delicious meal. When we were done, we gave the carcass to the gunner to throw out along the dirty streets of Ramadi, and we sat fat and happy for a few minutes as we rolled along in the Humvee to our next patrol area.

When the citizens were out in the streets, we'd attempt to talk to the ones who seemed friendly. Many times, the children would flock to us, which we didn't mind because, most of the time, even the mujahideen had enough heart not to attack when children were present. The children always wanted to know our names. When I first arrived, I would get frustrated because the local kids would laugh when I told them my name. It wasn't until one of our interpreters told me that my name, Josh, sounds similar to the Arabic word for chicken. I was basically running around the city of Ramadi, telling everyone I was "Chicken." Oh well, I had been called worse and, from then on, I enjoyed seeing the reactions when I'd introduce myself to locals. It was a fun icebreaker and typically got a laugh from those around.

Sometimes we'd set an ambush in an empty shop late at night. If the shop owner had food prepared for the next day and it smelled delicious, we'd usually find it and eat it. That wasn't great for their business or for our efforts to win hearts and minds, but we'd always leave them more than enough money in the same spot from where we took the food. One night we had a small firefight when we were in one of these bistros and had been eating flatbread prepared for the next day. We had to leave the restaurant quickly as we were under fire, but we still took the time to put some money in the bread area and put the chairs back on the table tops. Our senior Marines were always great about making sure we made things right. They'd say, while laughing, "Hurry the fuck up! We gotta go!"

The business owners most likely hated us for helping ourselves, but at the time we thought it was alright because we were paying for it. Many of the men who were fighting alongside me had been to war two other times, so I figured it was just the way we went about things. I never thought we could cause any harm or be creating new enemies, but it is highly likely this is exactly what we were doing.

PUC

The insurgents seemed to attack just as we were getting comfortable again and complacency set in. One afternoon in July, a small enemy unit ambushed us as we turned the corner of a small residential road. An insurgent popped around the corner of a house and began firing down the road in the direction we were traveling. A quick burst of rounds left the RPK machine gun he was firing, cracking around us, but not impacting anyone. I was in the back of our high-back Humvee, providing security for the vehicle, when I heard the shots. I turned around to see what was going on, ready to fire.

"Contact rear!" someone yelled, but as I turned around, no more rounds were coming in our direction. The next thing I heard was an explosion, and I saw a small plume of smoke coming from a house on the corner of the road, near where the shots came from.

It turned out that the insurgent's weapon had jammed after the first burst, he then retreated to the courtyard of the house on the corner. One of our Marines nearest him threw a grenade over the wall, attempting to blow up the insurgent. The only casualty from the grenade was some civilian kitchen that was damaged from the blast. After assessing for threats, we took a man that was at the house as a PUC. He was a military aged male and was in the house where we just had contact. It made sense for us to bring him back as a PUC. We cleared out the rest of the buildings near the ambush site to ensure no one else was waiting for us. With no other signs of another attack, we continued our patrol and returned to base with our PUC.

In late August, we happened to return to that same home where someone had thrown the grenade. It was late morning, around ten or eleven o'clock. We stood in the air-conditioned house and waited for the next squad to move across the street and clear a couple of houses so we could keep moving. A younger woman in her early twenties approached and looked up at me. She had pretty eyes but a terribly unsightly unibrow. She began talking to me in a very direct tone. Our interpreter was standing near me and began telling me the woman was upset we had taken her brother, that he was being held at Abu Ghraib. She wanted to know why he was there because she said he wasn't a terrorist. I told her he probably was a terrorist and that was why he was being held. Frustrated, she began to cry, speaking faster and with more pain in her voice. Again, I looked her in the eyes and told her, "Your brother, Ali Baba" (or bad guy, in the context that we had been using throughout our time in Iraq).

She began to sob and ask, "Why, why did you take my brother?"

I replied by laughing. I couldn't hold it back anymore. The callousness of the deployment was rearing its ugly head. I was staring at her unibrow and, as she became more frustrated, it moved, resembling a caterpillar. I was laughing so hard I had to leave her sobbing in the room and met back up with my squad in the living room.

Reflecting on that situation, a woman was standing before me, defeated and wondering where we took a member of her family. I replied to her pleas by accusing him of being a terrorist and laughing. Even if her brother was a terrorist, it wasn't right for me to deny her the humanity of listening to her concerns. It was once again another gauge of how much the combat changed me.

Sometimes, we were tasked with taking the interrogated PUCs from Camp Ramadi and Hurricane Point back into the city to set them free. We would do this under the cover of darkness. Many times, we'd just drop them off in the middle of the souk, leaving their hands zip-tied and heads covered with an empty sandbag to find their own way back home.

Once we actually broke a blue chem-light, or glow stick, and covered the man in a fluorescent blue chemical. When we dropped him off, he stood there and glowed blue on the dark street. Decisions like that had a long-lasting effect on our failure to win hearts and minds. The strategic lance corporal mindset works both ways, and we unknowingly caused our share of harm to the mission we were trying to accomplish.

CHAPTER 3

Brothers

We had heard of some of the other platoons in our company and battalion being blown up by improvised explosive devices (IEDs) and taking casualties, but we had yet to experience the true power of roadside bombs. I had seen IEDs explode on other patrols from my post at the Government Center and had been extremely lucky until April 19. On that day, we were returning from a raid in which our platoon had found some weapons caches. It was around eleven at night and my turn to use my M249 squad automatic weapon (SAW) to provide security for our high-back Humvee. That meant I had to put the bipod of the weapon on the roof of the cab while I sat on an MRE (meal, ready to eat) box in the center of the vehicle. Since we didn't have a proper seat, I turned the box on its side, resulting in a very precarious ride. The armor of the Humvee didn't cover my chest and head, leaving them exposed. Something had malfunctioned with my night vision goggles (NVGs), so I reached back and asked one of the other Marines for theirs so I could see better. After I traded with them, I turned back around to face the front. As our Humvee turned a corner, the same corner where Bravo Company's outpost was blown up a few weeks prior, a feeling of immense pressure overwhelmed me. I don't remember the explosion, but I remember coming to my senses. The smoke engulfed us as our driver sped down the road, continuing with the direction of movement. The IED detonated directly on the left side of our vehicle. I immediately started feeling my body, trying to see if anything was sticking out or missing. I found nothing, so I turned around to see what everyone else was doing. Cannan yelled, asking if anyone was hit. All of us in the back took turns announcing we were fine. Cannan reported to our platoon sergeant on his radio that everyone was okay. It was dark outside, which made it difficult to see anything, especially with the smoke that was still lingering in the back of the Humvee.

"Ah, fuck, I think I'm hit," Corporal Dunn begrudgingly said.

Cannan asked where.

"My foot," Dunn said calmly.

Mortenson pointed his flashlight at Dunn's foot; we all turned to look down at his boot. Smoke was coming from two small black holes, one on the side of his boot and the other by his big toe.

"Fuck. Aw, fuck, man. Fuck you, Iraq. Fuck you, Iraq!" Dunn said, all the while displaying his middle finger to the city as we drove by.

Mortenson grabbed his medical kit and pulled off Dunn's boot and sock. Blood spurted from Dunn's foot as Mortenson and another Marine did the best they could at bandaging it.

"Dude, your foot stinks, man," I said. It smelled like vomit and blood.

When we got back to our forward operating base (FOB), we dropped off Dunn at our battalion aid station (BAS). Two Marines helped him hobble into the BAS. That was the last time I saw him until I returned to the States. This being his third combat deployment to Iraq, it was nice to know he was getting out alive.

The next morning, we received word of a planned meeting of some high value targets (HVTs) near a gas station in a busy district of Ramadi. We spent the morning rehearsing for the afternoon's raid, which involved our platoon and 2nd Platoon. While we were doing our vehicle training, working on mounting and dismounting near the objective, Cannan noticed something different with our Humvee. It was the same one we were in the night prior, except for a small hole in the Kevlar blanketing that we sat on for more protection from roadside bombs. Also, our driver noticed shrapnel had punctured and destroyed the fire extinguisher sitting right under his seat. This was the cause for the majority of what we thought to be smoke that we kept breathing on the way back to our FOB. The small hole in the thick blanket was where Cannan was sitting the night before, between where his legs would have been. We pulled the heavy blanket back and discovered shrapnel had riddled the entire side of the vehicle. It had embedded into the blanket after passing through the Humvee. The one small piece that got through was most likely the one that hit Dunn in the foot. Cannan was amazed and happy the blanket was there. He kept on saying how lucky he was that the blanket saved his legs. He would have lost his legs; Dunn wouldn't have been the only casualty.

After we rehearsed for the raid, we spent the rest of the morning preparing our gear and talking around the smoke pit. Cannan was eating Goldfish crackers. He willingly shared them with some of us as he talked about camel spiders chasing Marines when the battalion was in Fallujah in 2004. Cannan, too, was a three-time Iraq veteran. The other 120-dayers were growing anxious as Dunn, one of them, had already been hit and was on his way home. Cannan confided in me that, a few days prior to April 19, he had told Sergeant Laws he didn't expect to make it home from this deployment. I told Cannan not to talk like that. He always mentioned casually that "third time's a charm," referring to the number of deployments and suggesting one can only escape getting injured so many times in combat before meeting with death or serious injury.

Around noon, the drivers staged the vehicles while the rest of us dismounted Marines made our way to our Humvees. We sat in the back of the same vehicle as the night before, still assessing the damage and being grateful for the Kevlar blanketing. We had cleaned the blood from Dunn's foot out of the back earlier in the morning, but we could still find spots where his enormous foot had spurted small droplets around. For this mission, it was Lance Corporal Joshua Arnett's turn to provide security for our vehicle with his SAW. He sat as I had the night before, bipod extended on top of the cab, sitting on an MRE box turned on its side. Lance Corporal Michael Tager, Mortenson, Cannan, and I all filled in the rest of the seats in the back of the high-back Humvee. I usually liked to sit nearest the rear doors, just in case we had to dismount quickly under fire. This way, I could provide covering fire with my SAW for the rest of my squad. When Arnett wasn't responsible for vehicle security, he would do the same. That day, for some reason, Mortenson insisted on sitting nearest the door, across from Cannan, who occupied the seat nearest to the other door. I was sitting just to the left of Cannan, and Tager sat across from me. I again reminded Mortenson that I usually sat nearest the door because I liked to have the option to shoot out the back if we needed.

"Shut your boot mouth and sit there," he said.

Then he smiled and offered me a piece of Doublemint gum. He always had a five pack of Doublemint stuck in the webbing on the front of his body armor. I took the gum, rolled the wrapper between my fingers, and flicked it onto the floor of the Humvee. I had always looked up to Mortenson as a mentor. Members of the platoon gave him nicknames like "Mad Dog Marty" and "Machine Gun Marty" because of his previous actions in Fallujah in 2004. He was very knowledgeable and respected. He also had a lazy eye that had been surgically fixed just before our deployment in Ramadi. We jokingly gave him a hard time about it until he got it fixed.

Just before one o'clock, we drove past the front guard post, departing Hurricane Point. Cannan flicked them off and yelled, "Fuck you, guard!" as he and Dunn had previously done, to give the Marines standing guard on Hurricane Point a hard time for having to be on post. It was friendly ribbing, as we were in positions similar to them at the Government Center during our rotations. Dunn and Cannan always yelled at them as we left the safety of the FOB, rubbing it in their faces that they weren't out patrolling with us.

We and the Hurricane Point guard Marines always maintained a bit of rivalry. Not that the guard Marines were any different from us. We just thought they didn't patrol as much as we did, even though most of us didn't have a clue what their schedule could have been.

We drove down Route Michigan, the main road through Ramadi, which had been the site of the IED from the night before. That day, April 20, I wasn't as happy-go-lucky as I usually was. Things felt different, especially since Dunn was gone. I was a lot more afraid of IEDs. My naivety had disappeared now I knew the power of these weapons. As we drove, our driver played music from rap artists the Ying Yang Twins on his portable speaker. The speaker sat between him and Sergeant Laws. Usually, we would sing along with this song, but today we quietly smoked our cigarettes and looked around at each other, keeping a little lower in the Humvee than we previously had. All of us held our breath and winced as we slowed to turn at Intersection 295 where we had been blown up the night before. We were ready to take another IED blast if they had one set up. My organs wrenched and I felt helpless as we passed the intersection.

But there was nothing; no explosion. Everyone let out a sigh of relief as we continued on toward our objective. We turned on a road that ran directly past the Government Center, to the south. The other Marines on post at the Government Center could easily see us as we drove by the road. The day prior I was told some people had amassed near the southeast corner of the Government Center, near an intersection of the road we were on and another we were driving toward. We didn't know the details of what had happened. Eventually, the Marines on post dispersed the crowd.

Civilians would always mass around the Government Center to gain entry. They would go to the government building and complain about their lack of electricity because one of our seven-ton trucks had ripped out power lines, or how they had lost their job because their shop was destroyed during a firefight. In order to speak to their governmental representatives, they would have to meet outside the wire and be accompanied inside by Marines. That day, as we drove by, no one was there to mass.

As we drove toward the intersection, I thought to myself, "That would be a great place to put an IED because we need to slow down significantly to get through the serpentine and continue down the road. Good thing we have guys watching it."

I looked at the guys in the back of the Humvee and arched my back to stretch and adjust my gear as we passed through the intersection. I only remember a white light. Not a light like someone would shine in your eyes, but similar to a photo that had been overexposed to light and washed out. Then everything went black. Someone had detonated another IED against us. The day before, a terrorist had hidden in that mass of people and placed a 155-millimeter artillery round on the backside of one of our concrete barriers, the ones we used to create a serpentine to slow traffic. When my vehicle, the third in the convoy and the first one with several Marines in the back, passed the barrier, the IED detonated. Since it wasn't buried, there was no obstacle to prevent the full force of the artillery round from reaching us. The concrete from the now-obliterated barrier hit the Humvee behind us, destroying its windows and the majority of its front end.

I initially felt nothing. Just blackness. Emptiness. No feelings. No senses. Complete brain system reset.

The first thing I felt was heat on the outside part of my left leg, near my knee. It burned badly. I began clumsily patting it with my hand. Shrapnel had hit my leg and was stuck to it, burning. I hadn't opened my eyes yet. My ears were ringing. I felt like I had been out drinking all night, the same feeling you get when you get too drunk, should have thrown up but didn't, and are now lying in your bed wishing you didn't have to wake up. I could hear myself breathing, but that's it. It felt like someone had put lead weights on my eyelids. They were heavy and difficult to open. I finally opened my eyes and everything was still. It felt as though an hour had passed as I drunkenly looked around the rear of the Humvee. I looked to my left and saw Arnett hunched over his SAW, his body very still. I glanced into the cab and saw Sergeant Laws lying against our driver, neither of them moving. Across from me, I glanced and noticed the top of Tager's helmet; he was slouched down, concealing his face. Next to him was Mortenson. His helmet was off and his chin was resting on his throat protector, almost looking directly at me. His eyes were closed. Blood ran from his head, covering his flak jacket, and his hands rested on his knees, palms up. I looked back at his head and still couldn't figure out why he wasn't wearing a helmet.

"This isn't happening, this isn't happening," I thought to myself, "Oh my God, I'm in a nightmare."

Then I looked to my right. Cannan was in the fetal position on the floor in front of the doors. When I reached down and tapped him on the right shoulder, I got no response. I reached out both hands and pulled him up between my legs. I noticed a little blood on the front of his flak jacket. By pulling back the right side of his throat protector, I discovered the source of the bleeding. A piece of shrapnel had punched a hole near his clavicle, spurting blood from his neck and on to me. I immediately shoved my fingers in the quarter-sized hole, trying to stop the blood. The pressure was so strong. His blood pushed its way through my fingers as I tried to reach into my med kit and pull out my Curlex gauze. I began screaming.

"Cannan and Marty are hit! Cannan and Marty are hit! We have two down!"

Arnett came to and worked his way to Mortenson to help him. Tager also woke up and was helping me grab supplies out of my med kit as I kept pressure on the quarter-sized hole.

"Get my fuckin', my fuckin', my fuckin'," I kept saying, struggling to find the words and pointing at my med kit with my left arm, desperately trying to tell Tager to get my Curlex bandage out of it.

I couldn't find the words I was looking for, but Tager opened my kit and gave me the Curlex. The pressure of the blood coming out of the wound was weakening, it wasn't spurting between my fingers anymore. I stuffed the Curlex into the hole and kept applying pressure, doing the best I could. There was no way I could stop the blood. It was the most helpless and frustrating feeling I had ever experienced. After handing me the Curlex, Tager stood up straight and then said, "I think I'm hit." He pulled a seven-by-three-inch piece of shrapnel out of his butt cheek.

He brought the shrapnel into my view, then startled and dropped it because it was still extremely hot. Our corpsman from 2nd Platoon, and "Doc" Jeff Lake, from ours, had finally arrived at the Humvee and were assessing both Mortenson and Cannan. I looked over at Mortenson. By this time, Arnett had already bandaged up Mortenson's head wound and was assessing him for other injuries. I looked down at my bloodied flak jacket and saw small pieces of pink all over it. Brain matter. Out of the corner of my eye I saw something sitting on the floor of the Humvee: a Kevlar helmet. One side of the helmet appeared to have exploded out, severing the chin strap. What happened to Mortenson then all made sense to me. Shrapnel had hit him in the head.

The designated casualty evacuation (casevac) high-back Humvee for this raid had backed up near our vehicle and was ready to be loaded up. I jumped out of the back of our Humvee while Doc Lake and Tager grabbed Cannan and put him in the back. When I landed on the ground, I couldn't keep my balance. I still felt drunk, and I stumbled around to come back to where Arnett and Mortenson were. Arnett helped put Mortenson over my shoulders and I carried him to the casevac vehicle. Tager had jumped into the back of it with us, but Sergeant Laws told him to get out to make way for Cannan and Mortenson. At that point, Laws didn't realize Tager was injured. Tager stepped out of the Humvee and, amid the casevac chaos, found himself remaining with the patrol.

I set Mortenson on the floor so I could jump in and sit on a cooler near the front to better support his head. Others helped as we slid Mortenson up, and we placed his head in my lap. He was still breathing. Our company first sergeant jumped in the back of the Humvee with us, and the driver took off. We had not closed the doors, and First Sergeant began to fall out of the back. I reached forward and grabbed him by the top front part of his flak jacket, pulling him in. We finally secured the doors and started making our way to the surgeons at the main medical facility at Camp Ramadi, Charlie Medical. Doc Lake had pulled Cannan's jacket open and was doing cardiopulmonary resuscitation (CPR) on him. I had my hands around Mortenson's head, cradling it. I had the right fingers of my hand near his throat, so I could be sure he was still breathing. Over all the noise, it was hard to hear if he was breathing okay. I could feel he had fluid in his throat, but he seemed to be still moving air in and out. His eyes were closed. Blood had pooled in them and coagulated between his eyelashes. I talked to him. "Stay with me, Marty, we're on our way to medical. You're gonna get help. Stay with me, Marty."

I stared at Cannan as Doc Lake continued CPR. I knew Cannan was gone. He bled out in my arms. His face looked so peaceful in death. He looked as though he was sleeping with a small smirk on his face. Time slowed down; I couldn't think straight. It seemed to take forever to get back to Camp Ramadi.

I looked at the little things around me. The blood in Marty's eyes. The helpless look on Doc's face. The blood-soaked Doublemint gum pack Marty had tucked away in the webbing of his flak jacket. We approached the front gate. Shouting about casualties, we all urged the

Army to hurry. We had to wait for the Army to move the tank used as a mobile barricade. We then sped through the camp and arrived at Charlie Medical, near the center of the camp.

As we stopped, the surgeons and other medical staff were ready for us. They ripped the doors of the Humvee open and I yelled, "Take this one. He's still breathing!"

The medics told me to remove his jacket as they put him on a stretcher. A second later, they loaded up Cannan and quickly moved him out of the Humvee and into surgery. It all happened so fast. I still hadn't processed what was going on. I jumped out of the Humvee and stood there, facing the other Marines in my platoon who went on the casevac. They were all staring at me. When I looked down, I saw I was covered in blood. Blood from my brothers covered me from my helmet to boots. Sergeant Sphoon came up and asked me if I was alright. I tried to breathe, but my lower lip quivered as my body went numb. Goosebumps appeared all over my body as I began to cry like I had never cried before. He hugged me, and I cried even harder. While glancing over near the chow hall, I noticed Arab workers standing outside of it, smoking and looking at us. My urge to kill all of them was intense. I wanted to end their lives. I couldn't believe what was happening. With the explosion having deafened me, the only thing I could really hear was the blood whooshing past my ears. My heart hurt. I sat down next to Arnett; a company support staff sergeant brought us new cammies to change into. We went into a room and talked with disbelief at what had happened. While changing into clean cammies, I observed that blood had left stains on my underwear around my groin. To confirm if I had been hit, I inspected my penis and scrotum, but there was nothing except drying blood, I suddenly realized the blood on my hands and crotch was from Marty's head as it rested in my lap. I checked my leg over and found a minor burn from where shrapnel had hit it, waking me up from my unconsciousness. I wasn't able to focus on my vision because I was crying again. With my mouth wide open, I tried to stop crying, and I blinked until the tears left my eyes. I walked back outside. There I learned Cannan had passed away and Mortenson was in critical condition. I didn't want to be in Iraq anymore. I didn't want to be alive anymore. Why wasn't it me who got killed? I felt I wasn't anywhere near the quality of Marine as Cannan or Mortenson were. It wasn't fair; it should have been me.

As we waited for Mortenson's helicopter to come and pick him up, we cleaned our gear and their gear. We had bristle brushes and water to scrub out the blood. We had to scrub all the blood off our gear so we could wear it again. It was at that moment that I suddenly realized I had left my SAW in the back of the Humvee we were blown up in. Sergeant Sphoon notified our platoon sergeant, who was still continuing on with the raid, and he replied he had accounted for it. I felt like a terrible Marine for having left my weapon and was beating myself up over such an irresponsible mistake. Everyone helped Arnett and me clean all four sets of the bloodied gear. We loaded Cannan's and Mortenson's gear into the Humvees and put our own wet armor back on.

We watched as a helicopter landed near the medical facility and the surgeons loaded Mortenson onto the flight. It took off and disappeared into the overcast and orange dusty sky. It all happened so fast. I was already in clean cammies, clean gear, ready to go back to Hurricane Point to await the return of the rest of our platoon for the next patrol. We got word the company had completed the raid mission and captured several terrorists. I felt lost in all the commotion.

The ride back to Hurricane Point was very lonely. Arnett and I sat quietly in the back of the Humvee as my ears rang; I knew I would never forget that day. I wished I was home with my family. I missed being naive and I was terrified to be back in a Humvee on the streets of Ramadi. We arrived at Hurricane Point. I entered the command post (CP) to collect myself and talk with our company Gunny. Captain Thompson and the rest of the Marines in the CP stared at us with a helpless look in their eyes. I don't remember anyone saying much of anything, except mourning our loss together in silence for those few minutes as Arnett and I dropped off Cannan's and Mortenson's body armor in the CP. We set it neatly along the wall. As I stood and stared again at Mortenson's disfigured helmet, I wished I could have done something more, wished I could have stopped Cannan from bleeding out in my arms, and wished I could just have a hug from my mom. I walked out of the CP as passing

Marines somberly told me they were sorry to hear about our loss. I didn't want anyone to say anything to me.

When the rest of our platoon returned from the raid, Arnett and I learned Tager had yet to receive medical treatment for his injury. He lay in the back of a high-back, on his chest, with his smiley face boxers pulled down, waiting for Doc Lake to escort him to Camp Ramadi for medical treatment. I thanked Tager for his help and told him I was sorry we left him behind on the casevac. With his southern Texas accent, he told me everything was good and not to worry.

Back at my barracks, I cried once more as I sat outside in the smoke pit with Arnett. I contemplated throwing out my tactical gloves that were soaked in blood, but realized I still needed them to protect my hands. While pouring hydrogen peroxide Doc gave me onto them, I sat and smoked a cigarette. I watched the peroxide foam red as it reacted with the blood soaked in my gloves. It mesmerized me. First, I would allow the foam to dissipate and the bubbling sounds to cease. Then, I would squeeze the blood out of the gloves and, once more, pour hydrogen peroxide onto them. I repeatedly performed this action until the foam changed its color from red to brown to off-white. I must have gone through a pack of smokes in the time it took me to clean my gloves. I sat outside by myself until the sun fell below the blood-red horizon.

Once the platoon had gathered and grieved for a short time, we had to inventory Cannan's and Mortenson's gear and personal belongings. The cartons of cigarettes they had stockpiled in their living area were divided between each of us. Boxes were filled with their belongings and transported to the CP to be sent back to their families. We placed the boxes next to their ripped-up body armor.

Later in the evening, the lieutenant (LT) gathered us all in the barracks. He had news about Mortenson. We all sat in a half circle as he told us Mortenson had passed away in the helicopter on the way to the hospital. I had felt he would not make it, but I didn't want to say it. I had still hoped I was wrong. Near the smoke pit, I walked out into the cool Iraqi night and joined my friend Lance Corporal Eric Young, one of Mortenson's closest companions and a veteran of the initial invasion and Fallujah. Again, we cried.

It was our platoon's turn to go to the Government Center the next morning. We loaded up our Humvees with supplies like Gatorade, food, and ammunition for our four-day stay and prepared our gear for the next morning.

The next day, I was back on the same post that I always sat; it overlooked the previous day's IED blast site. I sat up on the post, staring at the location where we had been blown up not even twenty-four hours before. People generally try to avoid situations that place them in close proximity to where a tragic loss or event occurred, yet there I was, unable to look away from the site where Mortenson and Cannan lost their lives. I stared at the blown-up concrete barrier and black marks where the IED was planted. Sergeant Laws came up to my post to check on me. I must have gone through three packs of cigarettes since the explosion the afternoon before. Sergeant Laws said I could fire off some rounds if I wanted to. I looked at him.

"What would that do?"

"I don't know, just thought it might feel good."

Rising from my post, I discharged around twenty rounds from my SAW into the intersection where Marty and Cannan had perished. I put my weapon back on safe and sat back inside my post, staring back out into the place where my whole life had changed. Sergeant Sphoon came up to my post and sat with me, smoked a couple cigarettes, and asked if I needed anything. I told him a drink and we both half-heartedly laughed. It seemed everyone was stopping by my post that morning. Not even twenty hours had passed, but it felt like an eternity. First Sergeant came up, gave me a couple of cigarettes, and smoked with me.

We looked at First Sergeant as "the Don." He wore dark-tinted aviator-style prescription glasses and had dark slicked-back hair. Had he not been a Marine, I'd have assumed he was from an Italian mafia family out east. When he talked, he sounded like the comedian Mitch Hedberg and, if he was looking at you, you might wonder if you did something wrong. He had a hilarious but very dry sense of humor that only got better the longer we stayed in Ramadi. We all respected yet feared the man.

One day, a guy from our platoon had his freshly washed cammies drying on a clothesline outside the hooch at Hurricane Point. First Sergeant walked by and saw a hole in one of the cammies. He didn't want us to walk around with holes in our cammies because it looked unsightly, so his fix was to stick his finger in the hole and rip it bigger, rendering the clothing unserviceable. Stuff like that frustrated us and made us fear him. We all wondered whose turn it was going to be to feel the wrath of First Sergeant.

Another day, in front of an Iraqi family, he yelled at one of our corpsmen for having his sleeves cuffed up, trying to stay cool while on patrol. I was right next to him when he began yelling. I slowly sneaked away, trying to make it look like I was holding security somewhere else. As I walked away, I made sure to look down and check all of my gear to make sure nothing was wrong with it, thereby preventing an ass chewing. He was also great at identifying Marines who had a paint-chipped black rank chevron, worn on the front of our flak jackets. If he noticed it while we were out patrolling the streets of Ramadi, he'd say, "Hey, dipshit, make sure you blacken your chevron when we get back."

I swear he made it his goal to come up with new things to call us to get our attention: "Hey, dumbass" or "Hey, fish-lips" or "Hey, needle dick." I always felt he was a good leader because he didn't care what we thought of him. He was watching out for our wellbeing and for the reputation of our unit. Every opportunity he had, he reminded us that discipline started at the lowest level. As a good Marine, he consistently reminded us we were Marines first, too. It was easy to fall for the darkness of combat that leads to poor discipline and decisions. He did his best to help hold the company together.

Back on post, First Sergeant told me to let him know if I needed anything. I told him I was alright and thanked him for stopping by. Our company commanding officer (CO), Captain Thompson, was the last person to come up to my post.

I had immense respect for our CO. Previously an enlisted Marine, he understood what it was like to be junior enlisted, which is why I had immense respect for him. He was an outstanding leader and a great man. I felt a sense of relief when I saw him enter my post, a sense of security in a way. He was older than a lot of the others in the company and carried a lot of wisdom with him. He brought up some coffee and sat with me. I thanked him and we sat in silence, sipping coffee for a period of time. I felt like I should be courteous and engage him in conversation, but then realized I really had nothing to say and just sat and stared at the IED site.

"If it helps at all, which I'm sure it won't," started Captain Thompson, "Cannan died right away when the IED went off."

"How do you know that?" I asked him. "He bled out in my arms. I felt the blood pump through my fingers when he was still alive."

"The surgeons told me that the shrapnel entered his shoulder where you saw and went directly into his heart," my CO said.

I sat for a moment, processing it all.

"Thanks, sir."

We talked for a while more about how messed up everything was, how it felt like I was in a nightmare; he told me to stay strong. I didn't want to let him down or cause him to doubt my ability to be combat-effective, so I stayed strong. He told me to be sure to let someone know if I wasn't feeling right and told me I could talk to him anytime if I needed anything. He told me to be sure to get some rest on my off time as well, that it would help with grieving.

Arnett and I weren't able to sleep for three of the four days at the Government Center. Every time I closed my eyes, I saw the faces of Cannan and Mortenson. I was afraid to shut my eyes. Instead of sleeping, I listened to music, smoked cigarettes, and drank coffee. Our corpsman instructed Arnett and me to just focus on sleep and finally gave us sleeping pills. We both slept for 18 hours straight. We needed that. When we woke, we found out Tager was going to be heading home. I felt happy for him. At least I knew he would make it home alive.

They transported Tager to Balad for surgery on the shrapnel wound in his backside. We had expected he'd have a safe return to the States so he could recover from the massive hole in his butt cheek.

A couple of us were standing outside the CP on Hurricane Point one night, a week or so later, when I heard a familiar voice.

"What's up, guys?" A voice with a southern accent came from the darkness as our faces reflected our delight.

Tager appeared from the rear of a recently arrived Humvee with a huge grin on his face. We were so happy to see him.

"We thought you were going home?"

He told us he was supposed to go home, but he couldn't leave us, so he escaped the hospital after his wound was treated and stumbled upon an Army convoy heading for Camp Ramadi. He asked the convoy commander if he could hitch a ride. The soldier didn't see why it would be an issue, and Tager was on his way back to Alpha Company, 1st Platoon. He was still healing, and he had to visit the surgeon on Camp Ramadi a couple times for the rest of the deployment to be sure he was healing properly, but he could patrol with us. The only adjustment he had to make was sitting on a pillow in the cradle of the machine-gun turret, to prevent his injury from hurting too much. Tager was a remarkable man for that decision. I don't know if I could have made the same one.

A couple of weeks after we lost Mortenson and Cannan, we left on yet another raid. I took on the gunner position in a Humvee for that night. We usually rotated the responsibilities of each squad for every patrol. It was my squad's turn to operate the machine guns on the vehicles. Around ten o'clock in the evening, we left for the company sized raid and positioned ourselves in our blocking positions. We passed two suspicious Iraqis who were sitting on the curb of the road. While driving past them, we yelled at them to go away, and they gradually stood up and left. In retrospect, I wish we could have killed them.

My vehicle pulled up and parked down the road where our position was to be held for the raid. Lance Corporal Garcia pulled the concertina wire off the hood of the Humvee to drag it across the road, blocking it from vehicular and foot traffic. Just then, we heard a large explosion near where we had driven by on the way to our current position. Over the radio, we heard a casualty report being given to battalion headquarters. An IED had hit someone. It was one of our company's seven-ton drivers, a lance corporal. I did not see him, but I later heard what had happened from a Marine that was there.

The IED had exploded on the driver's side, causing the vehicle's engine to stall. The driver immediately began trying to start his vehicle, having woken up from being knocked unconscious, and realizing the truck was not running. I heard he continued to keep trying to start it. First Sergeant walked to the driver's side of the vehicle and opened the door. The Marine was still trying to start the truck, but had a large piece of shrapnel sticking out the side of his head. Apparently, when he realized what was happening, he passed out.

For the rest of the deployment, we received updates on how he was doing back in the States. The last update I remember was that he could speak his name again and was relearning his ABCs. I wished he was better and hoped it wouldn't be me in the future.

The weapons company first sergeant would play "Amazing Grace" on his bagpipes whenever a Marine was killed in our battalion. He would walk around Hurricane Point playing the music. The Marine Corps authorized him to wear the Marine digital camouflage kilt, which he sometimes wore as he played. It was always difficult to hear "Amazing Grace" playing in the distance when relaxing in our hooch on Hurricane Point. It meant we had lost a Marine brother and that a family back home in America was about to have the worst day of their lives.

We would attend memorials for our fallen brothers while in Ramadi, and the first sergeant would be there playing the bagpipes, after which a rifle salute would take place outside of the memorial services, followed by the bugle call of "Taps."

For Cannan and Mortenson's memorial service, I carried Marty's boots to the front of the room to form the Battle Cross. Others from our platoon volunteered to carry the other items needed to form the cross—rifle, helmet, dog tags, and photograph. I always had a hard time at the memorial services, but I tried to make it to as many as I could for the fallen Marines. For example, our company took a small convoy to a neighboring FOB to attend Corporal Starr's memorial service, a Marine from Bravo company. He was killed on Memorial Day, and I remember thinking to myself, "They will inform his family on Memorial Day that their son was killed in action."

CHAPTER 4

The Grind

The Buying Power of the US Dollar

I didn't notice I was turning into a monster. Since everyone around me was also going through a similar transformation, noticing the changes taking place was difficult. Some people in our battalion were being investigated for doing things like zip-tying dead insurgents to the hoods of Humvees and parading them around the city, while others were pretending to get shot at so they could just shoot up people who were out and about. We were all losing our minds. It appeared there were too many rules for us to follow, all while so many of our guys were getting injured and killed. Our training focused on turning us into killers, not peacekeepers. It was around June 13 when I noticed how much Iraq had changed me. In only four months of combat, I was becoming someone I never wanted to be, let alone someone I would never have wanted to associate with back home.

We were on patrol in the evening, conducting information operations with a Civil Affairs Group (CAG) attachment. I was attached to another squad for this patrol—one with my good friend in it. The CAG officer needed a seat in the Humvee, so they bumped me from the truck with Lance Corporal Kenny Morgan and Sergeant Sphoon and put me in with another squad. We dismounted our vehicles, the same as we would have for any other patrol. We started clearing out the buildings next to our dismount locations to be sure no threats were waiting for us. I entered a house with several Marines and found an Iraqi family sitting in their living room. A woman, several girls, and a couple of young boys were huddled together in their home. We separated the males from the females because the woman wouldn't stop talking loudly. I noticed one young boy staring at us with hate burning in his eyes. He looked to be about twelve years old or so, old enough to understand what we were doing and what was going on in Ramadi. He was speaking Arabic; one of our guys in our platoon who was self-taught thought he knew what the kid was saying. He was certain he was saying something about how he liked to hear about Marines dying, how he hated Marines. I got very upset; I asked if he was sure that was what the kid was saying, and he replied he was pretty sure. While the rest of the Marines searched the house and stood guard over the family, I directed the boy to follow me and the other Marine into a room.

I immediately zip-tied the kid's hands behind his back. I towered over him. He was probably just over four feet tall. He panicked and spoke Arabic while I was zip-tying his hands and I told the other Marine to tell him to shut up. The kid would not shut his mouth. He was obviously upset that we were there, inside his house. I was getting frustrated that he wouldn't stop talking. He began saying he loved Marines, that there were "no Ali Baba Ramadi" (no bad guys in Ramadi) as he cried.

The Marine with me wasn't comfortable with how things were escalating and also commented he wasn't completely sure the kid was saying he didn't like us. Only then did I realize what I had just done to the poor kid. I turned him back around. Using my Gerber multi-tool, I cut the zip-ties from his hands and gave him five US dollars. Lamely, I felt that compensating the child would make amends for my recent actions. I was a moron and a bully. We opened the door to the living room; another Marine stood there and asked what we were doing. I told him we were taking care of a future terrorist. Looking back at it now, if I did anything, it was to convince the kid that Marines truly were bad people, that we were the monsters and terrorists in his country.

As soon as the kid went back into the room with his family, we heard gunfire outside. We ran to the windows to see what was going on. A voice announced over the radio, "Alpha Sierra [four numbers] has been shot."

Alpha was the infantry company designator, followed by the first letter of the individual's last name, and then the last four digits of their social security number. We were trying to figure out who else had a last name beginning with "S." I was okay, so were some others. We then heard Staff Sergeant Danny Santiago, "Papi," reporting on the radio calling for the casevac. As we were going through the rest of the "S" last names in our platoon, we received news over the radio that Sergeant Sphoon had been hit. A sniper had shot him in the wrist as he was tossing an orange road cone out into the road for a traffic-blocking position. The bullet entered his wrist and exited out his elbow. When the initial call came over the radio, however, it was misunderstood as a gunshot wound to the head.

The Charlie medical station was preparing for a head wound, when it really was an extremity wound. Once the casevac arrived at the medical station, the misunderstanding was cleared up. We gave him to the surgeons and then washed his bloody body armor and gear. Memories of Mortenson and Cannan came flooding back. I was terrified for Sergeant Sphoon. I looked up to him and thought he was invincible. He helped me so much through processing the losses of Cannan and Mortenson. Now he was wounded. When I went into the emergency room, I witnessed him all messed up, shaking, and breathing erratically. I wanted to cry but knew I couldn't. I didn't want him to be afraid or to have any more concern than he already had. With tears streaming down his face, he was apologizing. He wasn't crying because he was hurting; he was crying because he felt he had let us all down and was going to be away from us. I remember I told him, "See you soon, Sergeant Sphoon," touched his good arm and left the room.

He was a prominent leader. I was glad he was going home to his wife and kids. I was so happy he would make it out of Ramadi alive.

Sunflowers

On June 15, Papi woke us early in the morning, around 0230. In a very somber tone, Papi told all of us to get up. We all wondered what was going on.

"Second Platoon has been messed up, bad," he told us.

He then listed five names:

"Jamie, Trovillian, Maynard, Whitley, and Flores. All of them."

My heart dropped. I couldn't believe it.

The company held Trovillian and Jamie in high regard as combat veterans from Operations *Iraqi Freedom* 1 and 2. Jamie's twin brother was also in Alpha Company, though he was in a different platoon. Maynard went to the School of Infantry with me when we were young Marines. He was also the first person I met when I reported to Alpha Company. He was in the company office, on duty, because he had injured his leg during a training event. When I had arrived back in October 2004, the rest of the company was out training in the field, so he helped get me settled into the barracks. Whitley and Flores joined the Marines a little after me; I did not know them very well. Within the first week that I arrived at 1st Battalion, 5th Marine Regiment, and was assigned to Alpha Company, I met Trovillian.

My then roommate (another lance corporal) and I were sleeping when we awoke to a pounding at our barracks door.

"Get the fuck out here, boots!"

It was a senior lance corporal and Corporal Trovillian; they had been drinking. My roommate and I opened the door. We were in our boxers and it was cold outside. We were on the third deck of the barracks. Trovillian called for us to come out to talk to them, so we walked to where they were drinking on the walkway and stood at parade rest. The two of them then asked us if we wanted to kick their ass. We emphasized we did not want to cause any harm to them. The senior lance corporal explained Trovillian could destroy us because he was a Golden Glove boxer or something to that effect, which was intimidating, not only because he was a proven fighter but also because both guys had been in combat. Trovillian asked if I thought I could kick his ass because I was taller than him. I told him I didn't want to fight. They harassed us for a couple more minutes and then told us to go back to bed. I held no grudges against either of them. Being a "boot" comes with that territory, but they were some of the first Marines to mess with me when I arrived at Alpha Company.

The five Marines from 2nd Platoon had been blown up by an improvised explosive device (IED). Apparently, it was a very large and very hot explosion. I remember seeing 2nd Platoon return that morning, as we were preparing to go to the blast site and pull the disfigured weapons out of the back of one of their Humvees. Some rifles had been bent, some fused together because of the heat. I couldn't believe it. Our platoon received the task of providing security at the IED site to retrieve pieces of the Humvee and gear. We loaded up on our trucks and headed out to the scene after doing our best to give the members of 2nd Platoon our condolences.

When we arrived, we took up security in the houses surrounding the blast site. The crater from the IED was massive. I took up position to the east of the site. I sat on top of a building and looked out and away from the blast site. A while passed and, as expected, we took small-arms fire. We also heard some firing to the northeast. Rounds snapped across the rooftops and we hurried off the roof. It was hot that day; my boots were sticking to the tar that covered the roof we were on. I remember wishing my feet would move quicker, but the stickiness of the tar prevented my long stride from moving any faster. As we moved to the lower floors of the house, we learned Headquarters Company's Hospital Corpsman Second Class Baez had been shot in the neck while returning to his vehicle during the last exchange of gunfire. We watched his medical evacuation pass our position. The casualty evacuation Humvee rocked back and side to side as they drove as fast as they could get back to Charlie Medical. Unfortunately, he died on the way.

I was then told to move my position to one directly next to the explosion site. To get to the new position, I had to cross the blast site. I was afraid to go by it because of the massive loss of life. I moved across a sunflower field as I made my way to the other Marines from my platoon. The presence of a field of waist-high sunflowers was odd because much of the city was a dump and neglected. It wasn't a common sight, at least in our area of operations. Debris from the Humvee was strewn across the sunflower field, and the dark spots on the sunflower petals resembled blood. War has a way of ruining the beautiful things in life; the images of the sunflower field burned into my soul. I don't exactly know why—maybe it's because sunflowers are supposed to be pretty. Seeing blood on some of the sunflower petals ruined that beauty for me. To this day, whenever I see a sunflower, I'm brought back to that patch of land, strewn with the senseless loss of life. War turns the beautiful into the ghastly, the kind into the cruel.

As I neared the crater, I noticed pieces of Marine Corps digital cammies and destroyed gear, all blackened by the explosion. It was depressing to know my fellow Marines, guys who had trained me and with whom I had enjoyed meals, had once worn those pieces of clothing and gear now strewn about the area. Seeing the carnage surrounding the blast site, my heart ached for the Marines of 2nd Platoon.

I finally reached the building where the rest of my squad was and noticed brownish-red debris all over the courtyard of the building. About fifteen feet up on the wall of the house were marks that looked like someone had thrown a towel, wet with burgundy paint, against it. The wall to the north of the compound had a similar marking, not as large though. Another large mark sat just below the one on the wall. I stood there, still, looking around and feeling a crushing weight on my heart as I pieced it together in my mind. My thoughts were confirmed when I found out everything I was looking at had belonged to one of my Marine brothers. I wanted to look away, but everywhere I looked was a reminder of the horror from hours earlier. Even if I had closed my eyes, the smells of the burning and iron would have filled my nostrils, a way for the devil to tease and taunt combatants. I attempted to find some sort of peace with it so I could still focus on being in combat, but the deaths of five good men clouded my mind. Five brothers. Five sons. Five Marines.

We provided security at the blast site for a few more hours until our platoon came under sniper fire. A bullet impacted just above one of our turret gunners. He was in the turret of a Humvee behind his machine gun when the round impacted directly behind him, sending bullet fragments into his neck but not seriously wounding him. We were sitting ducks, so our command decided to leave. We loaded up, returned to Hurricane Point, and prepared for a company raid that was to take place that evening with 2nd Platoon. As we readied our gear for the raid, we heard the first sergeant's bagpipes begin to play "Amazing Grace." Tears came to my eyes as I remembered the number of times I'd heard the song in the previous four months.

Lead Feet

Following the loss of the five Marines in 2nd Platoon and "Doc" Baez, our platoon and 2nd Platoon were set to carry out an evening raid in the busy marketplace. We returned from the IED site in the afternoon and began preparing for the company sized raid. We were itching for a fight and wanted revenge for the loss of our comrades.

The raid was to take place on a busy street named Cinema, in the heart of the souk. We were searching for IED-making materials in that area after the company received a tip. Cinema boasted one of the tallest buildings in our area, around eight-stories high, and was also lined with many shops and restaurants. Large granite tiles covered the sidewalk and made for an upscale-looking shopping area. Our platoon was to take the west side of the street, 2nd Platoon the east side. We rehearsed the movement up to the objective back on Hurricane Point, a rehearsal that was generally for the drivers to feel comfortable with vehicle placement, but all of us took part in it. We departed for the objective area around 1500, with the news of our fallen brothers still fresh in our minds and weighing on our hearts.

Quietly seated, we reflected on the day's events as the seven-ton truck chugged along down Route Michigan. The loud engine and smell of diesel made for a hypnotic and somehow relaxing break in the moment's commotion. Many of us smoked, so we typically tried to get a few cigarettes in us while we rode in the back of the truck. Occasionally, a team leader would peer over the side of the seven-ton's walls to see what the streets looked like. If the streets were empty, we could expect a firefight or IED. If they were busy, that usually meant there would not be any enemy contact.

We pulled up to the objective and were given the order to dismount. We did this as quickly as possible because of our vulnerability to an ambush while mounting and dismounting. Once we had both feet on the ground, we'd run in different directions to keep from being easy targets. Although we had received fire from a sniper a few times while mounting or dismounting over the course of the deployment, we were fortunate this raid was not one of them.

Once my boots were on the ground, I began my run toward the sidewalks while searching for cover. The street was not completely empty, with several vehicles lining both sides. I felt uneasy about everything and made the decision to charge my M249 SAW (Squad Automatic Weapon) into weapon condition one by pulling the charging handle to the rear and sending it back forward, making it ready to fire with the flip of my safety. We SAW gunners usually patrolled with our weapons in condition three, which just involved laying the belt of ammunition on the feed tray of the weapon and closing the feed-tray cover. The M249 SAW fires from an open bolt position, so pulling the charging handle back locks the bolt to the rear and makes it ready to fire. When you pull the trigger, the bolt slams forward and fires a round, then returns to the open position. This makes for a potential safety hazard if the operator of the weapon is complacent, like the Marine earlier in the deployment who had the negligent discharge. I would only put the weapon in condition one when we had contact with the enemy or it seemed enemy contact was imminent. I learned to trust my gut in Iraq; my gut was telling me to prepare for a fight that evening.

We all successfully dismounted while the drivers positioned the vehicles into blocking positions (a machine gunner and a driver always remained with each vehicle in order for quick movement and security of the vehicle). Our team assembled inside one of the shops, a photo-development business. I was with Sergeant Laws, two corporals (one of them a combat engineer attachment), and Lance Corporal Tager. We entered the shop and conducted a hasty search of the building to ensure there were no immediate threats. The upstairs was full of miscellaneous photo supplies and looked very disorganized. Two Iraqi civilians, most likely the shop owner and his boy, were present. They greeted us with a wave, saying "Hello" and forcing a smile. We were moved back toward the front door when Sergeant Laws heard through his radio that we were going to move south to meet up with the rest of the squad, who were in another shop. Because of short supply, only the Marines in the leadership billets were given a personal radio so we juniors always had to ask what was being communicated back and forth.

We formed a single-file line at the door, one of our platoon's corporals first, Tager second, the engineer corporal third, me, and then Sergeant Laws. I could faintly hear some communication over Laws's headset. The rest of the squad was ready for us to move to them. The first in line took off to the south and the rest of us followed. I had just left the shop and turned to face south to follow the combat engineer as he moved down the sidewalk when the insurgents' bullets began tearing into the vehicles directly to my left.

A heavy amount of automatic gunfire poured into the street, ripping into the parked cars to my left and the buildings to my right. It felt like I was in the middle of a tunnel, being riddled with gunfire. I was just leaving the building, so I turned back toward the photo shop and took cover behind the service desk inside, alongside Sergeant Laws. The gunfire sounded like a torrential downpour on a tin roof, but amplified to a deafening roar. The snaps of rounds passing by the shop were accompanied by whizzes from ricochets caused by impacts with vehicles, ground, and buildings. Rocket-propelled grenades (RPG) were being fired by the insurgents and were impacting the surrounding buildings. It felt as though an hour had passed before Sergeant Laws and I looked out the storefront's large windows. Gripped by the intensity and destruction unfolding before us, we only sat for about ten seconds before bullets began impacting the windows of the shop. Unsure of where the enemy was located, Sergeant Laws and I both fired through the windows at the buildings across the streets. It seemed the most likely spot because of where the rounds seemed to impact the windows. My ears rang immediately after my first burst with the SAW. We didn't have any hearing protection, so the first burst of gunfire always hurt the most, especially if firing from inside a building. I let a couple more bursts go and realized I wasn't really shooting at anything; I was just scared and I knew I needed to conserve my ammunition. We also realized 2nd Platoon was most likely across the street and possibly on the second floor.

Sergeant Laws could not get radio contact with anyone else. Neither of us had a clue which building the gunfire was coming from. He decided we should try to get to a different position within the building, so we made our way up the stairs to the storage area. Before I left the comfort of the service desk, I remembered the two Iraqis in the shop and wondered where they had gone. I noticed a black curtain behind the service desk.

Only then did I realize someone could have easily killed us by us not keeping watch on them. I figured the shop owner and kid were behind the curtain. To have more control if I needed to fire from the hip, I positioned my weapon under my arm and reached out with my left hand to pull the curtain open. With my guard up, I was prepared to eliminate any potential enemy that could be hiding behind the curtain. I threw it to the left and immediately returned my left hand to the handgrip on the weapon. I was breathing heavily, my eyes were wide to take everything in, and I was standing tall before the two Iraqi civilians who now sat on the floor gripping each other in fear. The older man had the younger boy in his arms, in a very protective and vulnerable position. The man looked up at me.

"Mister, no," he said softly, extreme fear etched on his face and reflected in his voice.

I stood there and processed everything, being sure not to miss a threat.

"Mister, no!" he said more confidently, fearfully begging for his life, with my weapon still aimed at both him and the young boy.

"Stay!" I said and gestured with my left hand to keep down. The man nodded and looked back at the boy.

I made my way up the small flight of stairs to where Sergeant Laws was. The volley of gunfire was still present outside, and now I could hear our heavy vehicle-mounted machine guns opening fire. Sergeant Laws still could not get hold of anyone on the radio.

"What took you so long?" he asked.

I told him about the two people downstairs.

"Damn, dog, I forgot about them. Good thing you didn't," he said as we both smiled.

"We have to go find the other guys," he said, knowing we'd have to move back onto the street and meet up with the other Marines from 3rd Squad.

"Okay," I said, and we made our way back down the stairs. I looked back, waved goodbye to the shop owner and made my way to the door where Sergeant Laws was already standing.

"When there is another lull in the gunfire, we are going to run. Ready?" he said.

In my mind, I doubted our survival, but still replied yes.

I didn't think about home or my fiancée or my childhood in those moments. The image of being ripped to shreds by bullets or experiencing a slow and painful death out on the street alone came to mind. I was the most scared I had ever been in my life. The bullets were still impacting the cars and street just feet from where we stood. I felt sick, most likely from the dump of adrenaline catching up to me. I wished our communications had worked so we could figure out a better plan. Instead of just Sergeant Laws, I had hoped to be with more Marines to increase our chances of survival in any situation that awaited us. I started wondering if my gear was too heavy to run fast. My boots felt heavy. Everything felt heavy. That's when the incoming fire momentarily stopped.

Sergeant Laws took off running, and I was just behind him. I was running out the door and committed to whatever lay in wait for us. My eyes darted around to locate any enemy positions, and places I could use for cover. Tunnel vision. My view was obstructed by a lot of smoke from exploding RPGs and debris from gunfire. In an attempt to make myself a more difficult target, I started running in a small zig-zag pattern. It was surprising how slippery the tile sidewalk had become, with all the debris from the buildings scattered across it and with the soles of my boots caked with tar from earlier in the day. I slipped and fell in the open.

My world began to operate in slow motion. I watched as Sergeant Laws ran down the street.

"Wait!" I shouted, but my call fell on deaf ears.

I watched as the building at the "T" intersection of Michigan and Cinema exploded with the impacts from our truck-mounted Mk-19 40-millimeter automatic grenade launcher, Captain Thompson's vehicle. Sergeant Laws's silhouette caught my eye as it darted into a building. I scrambled to get to my knees and get a footing again as the enemy's gunfire picked up. As soon as I had my footing, I was moving to where I had watched him enter a shop. It felt like it took minutes to get there, but it was only seconds.

"Coming in! Shores coming in!" I screamed as I neared the door to the shop.

I plowed through a stack of Marines who were waiting near the door.

"Jesus, where were you? I thought you were hit!" Sergeant Laws exclaimed.

"I fucking fell. Thanks for looking back, asshole!" I replied.

We both smiled; a feeling of relief poured over me. I was now back with three of my lance-corporal peers. Four other corporals were also with us. The building where the shots originated was about 150 meters to our south. It overlooked Cinema and provided the shooters with an excellent vantage point to fire straight down the road. We could now get communications with the rest of the patrol, and we found out our platoon was getting ready to assault the building we were taking fire from. We first had to meet up with Lance Corporals Garcia, Arnett, Morgan, and another senior lance corporal, who were around the corner from our building, down an alley with a squad of other Marines from 1st Platoon.

Our new group made our way to where Garcia's team was. I met with Morgan, and we both moved up to the corner of the alley where we could see the building we were taking fire from. Gunfire was still being exchanged between the insurgents and Marines, but the fire rate had dropped drastically. I leaned around the corner to look at the building. Securely gripping my SAW against my right hip, I positioned myself on one knee. I began methodically firing from the hip, walking my tracer rounds into each window of the building. I watched as the rounds ripped apart frames holding the window's glass in place. Morgan was firing as well, looking for movement in any of the windows. Shaking my weapon while leaning back into cover, I wanted to hear how much ammunition I had left in my 200-round plastic drum. As I was running out, I decided to use up the remaining drum in order to replace it with a new one. I leaned back out and began firing. I didn't realize Morgan was right next to me; when I finished firing, he was leering at me.

"Thanks for fucking telling me you were going to shoot again. Now I'm deaf, asshole." I laughed at him and told him to stop being such a pussy.

I then pulled back from the corner to reload my weapon and allow someone else to fire. While I was reloading, we got word we were going to assault the building. That meant we had to cross the six lanes on Route Michigan and a median before we'd have access to the front of the building. We decided Garcia would head out first to lead us into the building. We all readied ourselves and got into a stack, ready to move.

"Now make sure you don't trip in the street, Shores," someone joked.

I just shook my head. The plan was that as soon as the vehicle guns began firing on the building, we would rush across the open area and make entry. We could see from our position that the metal front door had a few holes in it from a Mk-19, so we figured it would be easy to get inside.

The vehicles began their covering fire; Garcia led our assault. As soon as he reached the median of the road, the vehicles stopped firing to prevent a friendly fire incident. It was up to us now. We reached the door and Garcia made a good attempt at opening it, but it wouldn't budge. The rest of us made it up to the building, but no one had opened the door yet. We all lined up alongside the outside of the building, hoping no one was going to shoot us as we stood there. Garcia finally got the door open, and we all burst into the smoke-filled building. The smoke was so thick the light from our flashlights dissipated in the particles and made for worse visibility. The air tasted sweet, almost like a sweet cigar (cordite from the 40-millimeter rounds). We all began to cough as we made our way into the building that we discovered was a bank. I located the stairs at the back, and we made our way up. Upon reaching the second floor, I discovered a spacious open area with small rooms encircling the perimeter. As I looked around the building, I began my search for anyone hiding. We couldn't find anyone inside. Our eyes caught sight of spent shell casings and trash. We knew they had been there, but they had left out the back. Captain Thompson, coughing, informed us we were going to check the mosque located just to the west. We all met up back by the door. Once we breached the gate, we readied ourselves to proceed toward the mosque. A lot of Marines filled that room. Even Captain Thompson was in on the fight. Garcia and Arnett had flashbangs ready for our movement into the mosque.

We violently exited the bank and made the 75-meter sprint to the mosque's gate, which was also located off of Route Michigan. As we ran, we saw an Iraqi man standing in the mosque's courtyard. Garcia and Arnett both quickly deployed their flashbangs near the man. As the devices exploded, we made entry into the main courtyard area. The now disoriented Iraqi man stood stunned as Garcia and Arnett took him to the ground and zip-tied his hands. My team continued moving past and made our way to the easternmost building in the compound. We quickly cleared out the one-roomed building and found nothing. Morgan and I began coughing up small amounts of blood. Morgan was coughing worse than I, almost to the point of vomiting. The residue from the exploded 40-millimeter rounds that had blasted the bank moments before was now settling in our lungs. It felt like I had smoked six packs of cigarettes. I couldn't catch my breath. Our team made our way into the outhouse part of the mosque.

Many toilets lined both sides of the small, hallway like bathroom area. About ten stalls were situated on either side of the walkway. Metal doors allowed access to a small three-by-three-foot toilet hole. The metal doors opened inward and were flimsy and noisy. Morgan and I began kicking open every door, checking for people inside. We made our way down, coughing the whole time, and found nothing. Once again, my gut was telling me something didn't feel right.

"You find anything?" our team leader asked.

"No, it's good," Morgan replied.

"Okay, let's go check that building," our team leader gestured toward another building that needed searching in the compound.

"Wait. Morgan, did you check behind the doors?" I asked.

"No, did you?"

"No. Hey, wait up. We need to check these again." I called.

"They're small fucking bathrooms, man, you looked in all of them," our team leader impatiently said.

"It'll take a second!" I shouted and began reopening all the stalls and peeking behind the doors.

There wasn't much room, but someone small could have hidden behind the doors. I pushed one of the doors open and happened to look down.

High-back Humvee patrolling the market area in Ramadi.

Marines resting in "The Dungeon" of the Government Center in between patrols.

Marines from 1st Platoon dismounting on a busy street in Ramadi while on patrol.

Marines from 1st Platoon seen documenting information after capturing insurgents who were engaging them in a firefight.

Marines from 1st Platoon on patrol.

Photo taken by the author of the damaged Army Bradley.

Marines from 1st Platoon at the staging area on Hurricane Point, getting ready to leave for patrol.

Photo of the damage to the Humvee on the night of April 19, 2005.

The author on the far right, Garcia sitting next to him. Cannan on the far left with his helmet on. All members are from 1st Squad, 1st Platoon.

Lance Corporal Garcia (left) and Corporals Cannan and Dunn (center and right) in the main level of the bank after our first firefight.

Marty Mortenson in "The Dungeon" at the Government Center, staging for a patrol.

The author posing while on patrol with his SAW.

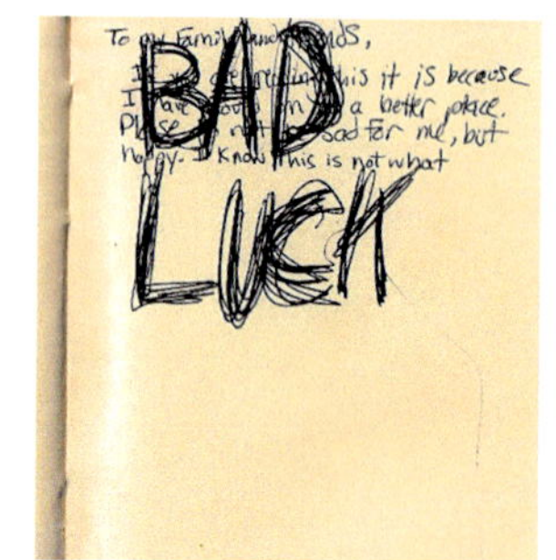

A page from the author's leather-bound journal gifted to him by his sister. This was written on the final page of the journal in the middle of the deployment, when the author felt he wasn't going to return home. It was crossed out because he felt it was bad luck to write a death letter.

A view from the roof of the Government Center looking out to the east.

Cammie netting set up to conceal movement along the Government Center's roof.

The author, left, with Lance Corporal Young, after dislocating his shoulder.

Members of the new 1st Platoon patrolling the jungle of Okinawa during training.

The flight deck of USS *Juneau* while at sea.

The author posing for a photo while training for deployment.

The author standing next to his Humvee after staying the night in the desert somewhere in Helmand Province.

That's when I noticed sandaled toes scrunched up, almost toe to toe with my boots, trying to stay behind the flimsy metal door.

"Hey, motherfucker!" With a yell, I pinned the person between the door and the wall of the stall.

"I found one!" I shouted to Morgan, who was now by my side.

"Watch me, man," I ordered Morgan.

"Gotcha," Morgan said as he stood in a position to allow for him to shoot if needed.

With my arm extended, I reached into the narrow gap between the open edge of the door and the wall. I violently grabbed for anything, finally getting hold of the man's shirt. I yanked as hard as I could, pulling an older man out from behind the door and into my view.

"Come here, motherfucker!" I shouted.

Using both hands, I forcefully pulled him close to me. I felt the weight of him grow heavy; he looked as though he were already defeated.

"What are you hiding from, asshole? You're mine now!" I yelled.

"Nice man! Good call," Morgan said.

"Maybe if you would have done it right the first time, we wouldn't have to be here now," joked our team leader.

I turned the man toward the entrance of the stalls and shoved him as hard as I could. He stumbled and fell on his face. Morgan reached down and picked him up, placed him in a restraining hold, and walked him to our collection point where he was zip-tied and put with the others we had detained. We went back and found another man in the bathroom area as well. That night we detained a handful of Iraqis who turned out to be insurgents or working with them. I was happy we didn't have any more casualties after such a terrible day. At least we found some people that evening, who could have potentially killed more US personnel, and removed them from the streets.

CHAPTER 5

A Fool's Heart

July 12, 2005, was the last entry I made in the leather-bound journal my sister had given me for Christmas. The journal had accompanied me throughout my deployment to Ramadi. I'd write in it when I had the time, documenting what had been happening on the deployment. Near the middle of July, I became convinced I would not make it home, and I found continuing to write in the journal more of a nuisance than cathartic. I wanted to climb into a shell and die. The anticipation of death made me impatient and aggravated that my ticket wasn't being punched. I wanted to die so I could lessen the anxiety of wondering when and how it was going to happen. In my mind, the best way to prepare myself for my inevitable death was to shut out my friends and family back home. I didn't want to hurt or surprise the people who knew me with my death, especially considering how the war was going. My only wish was for them to be okay with it and accept it, just as I had come to accept it. I didn't understand how other people back home couldn't grasp that accepting my death was one of the ways I coped with simply getting through the day.

In mid-July, I called my fiancée back home and called off our wedding. She was devastated, but I assured her it was for the best. Not feeling much of anything, after ending the phone call, I sat in the phone trailer. I didn't feel like I should regret what I had just done; I didn't feel empty. I somehow felt at ease. After calling her, I made another call to my parents to inform them of the same news. My mom thought I should wait until I got home before I made such a rash decision. I knew at the time she was most likely correct, but I felt the need to be understood at home, like I was understood in Iraq. I needed to be sure the people back home understood it wasn't because of anything they had done; rather, the changes in me had driven this decision. When I made the phone calls, I was sure to do it the night before our four-day trip to the Government Center. That way I wouldn't be able to talk to my family for another four days. I wanted to sit with my decision without being able to call and apologize. I wanted to hurt and yearned to feel anything.

While at the Government Center, I had a conversation with some of the guys in my platoon about my choice to call off my engagement. Through our talking and their leveling of how we all had changed, I realized I needed to keep the wedding on. I was acting out of fear and despair. They convinced me that when I got home and saw my fiancée, I would immediately want to be married and would regret the decision I had made. I agreed with them; when I returned from the Government Center four days later, I called my parents to tell them I thought I had made a mistake. They understood. They told me I needed to call my fiancée to be sure she was okay. When I called and talked with her, she was understandably upset. She couldn't understand how I could treat her like that, especially with all the support she had given me throughout the deployment until that point. I apologized and explained my flawed reasoning, blaming it on fatigue and the craziness of the weeks leading up to that point. She forgave me. We've been married since October 2005. I can't imagine my life without her.

Non-Potable Water

The summer months brought extreme heat, typically reaching above 120 degrees Fahrenheit. We would do our best to conserve our water on those hot days. We always had Gatorade and water in the back of the Humvees, but it would heat up within an hour of being out on patrol. There was nothing worse than trying to sip on hot red Gatorade. It seemed to dehydrate us more than anything. The bottled water was also hot and disgusting. We would patrol with coolers and ice sometimes, but that was usually the first to be consumed and was gone by the end of the patrol.

This particular hot August day, we were returning from a patrol, and I had just finished drinking the water from my Camelback on our way back to Hurricane Point. As we neared the gates to Hurricane Point, we saw M1A1 tanks and Bradley fighting vehicles traveling in the opposite direction along Route Michigan. I knew something was up. We rarely saw this amount of heavy armor rolling down the street. As we watched, some of America's largest mobile firepower swiftly passed by. When we reached the gate of Hurricane Point, we followed the roundabout just outside and returned to the city, following the heavy armor. I looked at the gate to the forward operating base (FOB) and wished I hadn't just chugged the remainder of my water. We were all concerned as we were low on water and exhausted. Most of us had finished the water we carried on us and knew we had no more. We drove far along Route Michigan and entered the Army's area of operations, which was in the eastern part of the city near a FOB called Combat Outpost. I had never traveled that far along Route Michigan and we were all trying to figure out what was going on. As we pulled up near Combat Outpost, we could see what was happening.

One of the Army's posts, located on the top of a high-rise building, had been partially blown up by a suicide bomber. The lower part of the building was on fire, and the westernmost part of it looked like it had collapsed. Tank and Bradley gunfire erupted around us as we took small-arms fire from the buildings around the Army FOB.

"We're helping the Army clear these buildings," one of our team leaders ordered. That's really the only warning order we received prior to dismounting our seven-ton trucks.

The driver pulled up next to a high rise across the street from the destroyed Army outpost and we began dismounting. A white-and-orange taxi, a staple for the area, sat in an odd position near where we dismounted. I hoped it wasn't a vehicle-borne improvised explosive device (VBIED) and hesitantly ran past it, looking for anything out of the ordinary. My team entered the high-rise building nearest our dismount location and began clearing it out, room by room. Trash and debris lay everywhere from where the tanks had blasted the building. Rounds continued to snap and whiz in the area. With my M249 squad automatic weapon (SAW) ready to blast the enemy on the other side of the flimsy residential doors, I did my best to swiftly clear the rooms. I was terrified and felt as though my heart would have beat out of my chest were it not for my body armor holding it in. I thought I was going to be shot up upon opening the door to the many apartments we searched that day. This late into the deployment, we were working off low reserves for manpower, so we found ourselves self-clearing several rooms. I believed I would die that afternoon. With every door came more hesitation but, with the success of surviving, clearing each room brought more confidence. The part of my brain that would have made for rational thinking went numb and the Marine in me took over. My weapon led me through the doors, ready to fire at any enemy that stood on the other side of it. My team made it to the top of the structure and found nothing. We ran down the flights of stairs to return to the street and moved south to an overwatch position a block south of the destroyed Army outpost.

There, we found a tall residential building and told the man and his young son who lived there to leave. We cleared out the house and took up an overwatch position on the roof. The area had a great view. The Army pulled their dead and wounded out of the debris from the destroyed outpost, loading them into Humvees as we watched. Seeing more Americans killed and wounded left a bad taste in my mouth. The scorching sun beat down on us on the rooftop as we did our best to change locations on the roof to avoid being easy sniper targets. An hour or so went by before I requested to change positions with another Marine. One of the guys from my squad relieved me so I could go to the bathroom and return to a new overwatch position. I walked down from the roof to the second floor and found a bedroom. I stood in the doorway to the bedroom and looked at all the broken glass lying around. When the VBIED that blew up the Army post went off, the overpressure from the blast broke all the glass in the buildings surrounding it. I don't know what compelled me to do this, but I walked up to the bed and pulled the covers back. Placing my SAW by my side, I secured it under my right arm. I reached down, unbuttoned my trousers and began urinating on the owner's bed, making a point of urinating all over it. At that time, a Marine who was going to the roof walked by the bedroom and stopped. He stood there and watched me.

"What are you doing?"

"Taking a piss," I replied.

"Why are you pissing on his bed?" he asked, continuing to stand in the doorway to the bedroom.

"Why not?" I replied without looking up, continuing to pee.

That seemed to be a good enough answer for him.

"Do you have any more water?" he asked.

"Nope, you?" I answered, as I finished urinating and buttoned myself back up.

"Nope," he replied as he turned and his voice trailed him to the roof.

I walked down to the first floor and met up with another guy from my squad. We looked in the freezer that sat covered in glass from the window next to it. There wasn't a thing in it. We were hungry and thirsty. The heat had deprived our bodies of almost all liquid. My body stopped sweating and I had a splitting headache. I walked out into the driveway of the residence because I heard a Humvee nearby. The vehicle pulled up and an officer from another company got out and walked over to us.

"How's it going, sir?" I asked him.

"Terrible, I'm fucking thirsty," he said.

"We are too. You guys don't have any water, do you?" I asked him.

"No, just some that is probably boiling in the back."

"Yeah, we're good without that. Do you know if we're getting a resupply at all?" I asked.

"I don't think so, guys, sorry. Everyone's really busy throughout the city."

"Okay" I replied.

"Good luck, guys," said the officer.

"You too, sir," I said as I watched him sluggishly walk back over to the Humvee with the rest of his Marines, who looked just as concerned as the rest of us.

As I turned around, I noticed a large metal salad-type bowl sitting under a dripping waterspout that was coming out of the side of the home we were at. The waterspout was like the ones we had back home for a garden hose. The intelligent part of me cautioned that I shouldn't drink it, but my body begged otherwise. I kneeled and opened the spout, letting the water from the city of Ramadi's supply run out into the overflowing bowl. I looked at the water to check if it had any discoloration or debris. It looked clear enough to me. I shut the water off and placed my mouth under the spout. I opened the spout and let the water flow. It tasted so good; it was even cold. I took enough water to quench my thirst, then told the guys on the first floor with me about the spout. Some took turns drinking some water, others refused, saying they didn't want to get sick. I didn't care. I needed water; the bonus came when I never got sick.

Back on the roof, I let everyone know about the water supply I discovered. I traded places with one of the Marines so he could go get a drink. We watched as an Army Bradley moved down the street toward where we initially got dropped off by our seven-ton truck. The Army suspected the lone taxi we dismounted directly next to was another VBIED. We watched in amazement as the Bradley fired its 25-millimeter main gun at the parked car. The first burst didn't produce any results other than ripping the taxi apart a bit. The second burst hit the warheads of the munitions loaded into the vehicle's trunk and produced a massive explosion. I don't know what was more deafening, the explosion or the cheers from all of us as we watched the bomb meant for us disintegrate into black smoke. I was beyond discouraged, though, knowing I was within ten meters of the taxi when we first arrived and hadn't been more vocal about my suspicions. My gut told me it was a VBIED, and it was right. War was honing my intuition. I just needed to heed it.

The Army removed the rest of the supplies and gear they needed from the outpost after dealing with the second suspected VBIED. They departed, and we broke down our gear and left our overwatch position to make our way back to the truck. We had been there for over four hours and had been patrolling the city for six hours prior to that. We were ready to get back to Hurricane Point and get resupplied on water and food.

I still wonder why I urinated on the bed of the Iraqi family, whether it was immaturity or numbness from combat or, most likely, a cruel mixture of both. I'm embarrassed it happened, and I hesitated to write about it in this memoir. However, I believe it's important to bring that memory to light. My mention of it is a vain attempt to seek forgiveness and to show the mentality of many of us during that stage of the war. I'm disappointed in my 19-year-old self, but not speaking of it and attempting to hide the injustices the Iraqi people endured only continues to divide.

CHAPTER 6

The Government Center

Countless firefights took place at the Government Center, a large building in the center of the city that was a magnet for bullets and explosives. During their four-day periods at the Government Center, almost every platoon was in a firefight of some sort. Whenever a firefight broke out, it typically involved volleys of small-arms fire back and forth, accompanied by mortars and the occasional rocket-propelled grenade to add to the chaos. We'd respond with a wall of bullets blasting from almost every post to establish a higher volume of fire. I recall shooting up every window I could see in one of the firefights as the enemy's fire rained on us, hoping one of the windows had the enemy in it. Knowing exactly where the combatants were shooting from was difficult, especially in an environment like a large city. It offered so many locations to hide and shoot from that a person could go crazy trying to pinpoint it. Once, when a firefight was over, an old man came out from his home, looked up at his windows, and looked back at me. He raised both fists in the air and shook them at me, storming back into his home.

I couldn't believe the insurgents would attack such a fortified position. If I had a choice between being on patrol or at the Government Center during a firefight, I much preferred the latter. I always felt a little safer when we'd fight there than when we were out patrolling. We had control over a lot more of the battlespace, and the fight was more on our terms. Every time we received enemy fire, we would get a high off our body's adrenaline rush, and each time it got easier to control. This was a lethal combination for anyone who attacked us. Some battles lasted only a few minutes, some lasted hours.

At one point, we had fired so many rounds that our ammunition supply ran low. Empty brass shell casings covered the roof of the Government Center. Luckily, an Army engineer unit had stopped by for the evening and was resting inside the building during the firefight. The soldiers all stayed in the safety of the Government Center while we Marines fought from the rooftop and standalone posts. The soldiers helped us by collecting all of their full AR magazines and dropping them into boxes for us to shoot. They dropped a large box in the center of the roof, overflowing with magazines. It was like Christmas for Marine infantrymen, with the tree being the camouflage netting covering the roof and the box of magazines the gift under it. I grabbed several of the magazines and used them in my squad automatic weapon (SAW), having to hold them in the magazine port as I emptied rounds into windows of buildings where I thought we were receiving fire from. I never thought I would run out of linked 5.56 ammo, but I did that evening. It felt as though the entire city was fighting us. I kept wondering where the enemy was getting their ammunition from.

Bullets were strafing across the top of the Government Center, pinging off the aluminum poles holding up the camouflage netting. I didn't dare put my head above the sandbag wall that lined the roof, as I usually did, as the volume of incoming fire was too great. During a lull in fire from the enemy, there was an awesome display of American firepower that night as Bradley armored fighting vehicles rolled in and began destroying buildings that had insurgents in them. Those, along with M1A1 Abrams tanks, pummeled the area and blew almost perfectly round holes into the sides of buildings. I remember being surprised at how near perfect the shell holes were in the buildings. Aircraft were conducting a show of force doing flybys over the city as well, diving from all around and tearing through the air with the sound of their afterburners. I worried the insurgents had outnumbered us, but when the heavy armor and air support showed up, they disappeared.

Some days we went through hours of nonstop battle. Many times we'd shoot until we were low on ammunition, never wanting to fire all the rounds available to us. I always carried a magazine with 28 rounds in my Camelback pocket, just in case I needed one last fighting option. We would unleash unrelenting gunfire there, covering the roof of the building with empty brass casings. At times I shot over 1,200 rounds in an evening. That amount of shooting from a small room deafens you for days. We didn't have hearing protection so if it became too painful, I'd find empty brass that had cooled enough lying on the floor of my post to stuff into my ears. A vain attempt at protecting my hearing at the cost of looking ridiculous. My mind became hypnotized by the rhythmic sound of my SAW chugging through the 5.56 linked ammunition. Tager and I would frequently be on the southern posts of the Government Center together. The incoming fire seemed to come from every direction. One day, his post, only about ten meters from me, was taking a lot more accurate fire than mine. I looked at him through the doorway from my sandbag post, into his concrete post, thinking how odd it was that he was the one getting the concentration of fire. He hunkered down while the bullets tore up the concrete around his post. He didn't look too terrified because he knew he was safe if he just stayed low.

"Shores! Gimme a hand over here!" he pleaded.

I stopped firing and tried to make my way across the roof. Bullets tore through the poles holding up the cammie netting, making loud pinging sounds alongside the snap of bullets passing close by. I dropped to the ground and crawled back to my post.

"Fuck you, man, I'm taking a lot of fire here, too!" I shouted. "Sorry, man!"

I fired my SAW blind over the sandbags for a few bursts, just to show the enemy I was still there. When the enemy's fire momentarily subsided, we both popped over the sandbags and returned fire. We didn't know what we were shooting at, but we wanted to make a statement that we were still around. The enemy had some advantageous spots to shoot at us from, so we'd fire at where we thought they were or where we knew they had used as fighting positions in the past. Often, we didn't know if we killed anyone; we just assumed we did because the gunfire would stop or slow down.

In the evening especially, we would get sporadic sniper fire at the Government Center. We would return fire and hope to hit whatever we were shooting at. I can't tell you how many palm fronds I shot over there, probably ten or so. I know I'm not the only one. Viewed from a distance, and with the right light, a palm frond looks like a person on top of a building, moving back and forth or bobbing up and down, depending on the wind. I recall a group of us shooting at a "guy on a roof," getting frustrated that he continued to show himself. It wasn't until we realized it was a palm frond that we ceased fire. I often laugh to myself at how ridiculous that would have looked. A group of Marines suppressing a leaf that just wouldn't stop taunting them.

War loves to tear at the mind of the participants. I recall Mortenson calling over the radio one night from his post early in the deployment. The exchange over the radio went something similar to this:

"SOG, this is post Bravo," Mortenson said.

"Send it," said the sergeant of the guard (SOG).

"I have a ... person standing outside the school looking at my post, over."

"Does he have a weapon?" asked the SOG.

"I can't tell. It looks like he's just staring at our post, though," claimed Mortenson.

Long pause.

"Fire some warning shots at him," suggested the SOG.

A few warning shots ripped through the chilly night air.

"He's still standing there. I'm going to shoot him," Mortenson said on the radio.

A few more gunshots disturbed the silent night as the rest of us on post sat intently waiting to hear what happened.

"SOG, this is post Bravo, disregard my last message ... the person standing there was a statue," Mortenson said over the radio.

Sheepishly, his words were carried over the radio, and laughter could be heard throughout the other Government Center posts. For the rest of the time remaining on post that night, other posts would call in to

Mortenson, asking if the man was still standing there. It was hilarious. In the morning, we all wandered down to look at the statue. It was of a child that stood on a pedestal in the courtyard of a school, full of bullet holes. Judging by the amount of damage the statue had taken, it looked like Mortenson wasn't the first to think it was a person.

Indirect fire was all too common at the Government Center and would come without the accompaniment of small-arms fire. We would sometimes hear the rounds leaving the mortar tubes, to which we'd alert everyone by calling "Incoming!" We'd sit in our post and wait for the impacts, looking around while wincing in anticipation of the rounds landing. We celebrated the Fourth of July while on post that year and the cooks brought us out steak and lobster for dinner. We could smell the grills cooking in the staging area of the compound. I was surprised we never received any indirect fire that day, with all the cooking and celebration at the Government Center. We even popped illumination rounds into the sky at night so we could see fireworks. Though the quality of steak and lobster was questionable, the whole dinner was extraordinary given our circumstances.

While sitting on post on a hot afternoon sometime later, I heard the announcement of incoming. I braced for the impact as a mortar round came so close to my post that I felt the overpressure as it dropped past and impacted on the ground below. I felt a quick vacuum as the air in my post was sucked out, followed by an immense pressure as the air returned with the concussion of the round's impact. Smoke filled my post and the post across from me. I thought the Marine next to me got hit with all the smoke and debris around. The thickness of the smoke prevented me from seeing into his post, like I usually could. I got up and ran over, finding him hunkered down, still smoking a cigarette. He looked up at me.

"I'm good, you good?" he asked.

I told him I was good and returned to my post, where I sat bored for the rest of that shift.

When we first arrived at the Government Center, the building had no working plumbing. All we had for bathrooms was the "Vietnam Shitter," as we called it—a 50-gallon steel drum cut in half and set under a plywood-constructed box with a toilet seat affixed to the top of it. To go to the bathroom, we would have to don all our body armor and walk outside to the courtyard to sit behind a wall of concrete blocks. The blocks were there in a feeble attempt to protect us if we got mortared, which I've established at this point was a regular occurrence. Once we got to the concrete wall, we would try to go to the bathroom as fast as possible, for fear of mortar rounds or, worse, flies. Nothing was worse than having one of the hundreds of flies walking around your nether regions while trying to use the bathroom.

Once the container under the plywood was full, usually in a couple of days, the team leaders would assign two unlucky Marines to pull the metal drum out of the box, using the hastily cut metal rim as handles to drag it 20 feet to a designated area to set it ablaze. We would have to pour diesel fuel into the drum and set it on fire. We monitored it for around forty-five minutes and took turns stirring it with a long stick to ensure all of it burned. When we finished burning everything down, small fibers of ash would cover us, and we would smell something similar to burned almonds. All of the "boots" had a turn burning the shitters and, lucky for me, some individuals regularly volunteered for the duty by acting like idiots, so I rarely had to take part in this necessary duty.

To keep from being bored while off post and still on our rotation at the Government Center, one of our corporals and Doc Lake did a lot of repairs to the building. They rewired our entire living area so we could have reliable power outlets. Those two guys were amazing. The efforts they put in to make improvements in our area went well beyond those of the combat engineers. They would also fix the vehicles that sat broken within the confines of the Government Center. By fixing a Mitsubishi sedan, they could drive from post to post within the compound. That car is how I learned to drive a manual. The handy corporal loved working on vehicles and was a skilled teacher. He enjoyed teaching me to drive stick while the other guys gave me shit, watching the car stall. Guys would drive around and do burnouts while the rest of us watched from our posts. Other guys, like yet another corporal, would find ways to keep our morale up. He played guitar, along with me and Young, while we were at the hooch on Hurricane Point. One night, at the Government

Center, he figured out how to work a public address (PA) system that had previously not worked at the compound. The sound it produced was extremely loud, as it had been used to send messages throughout the city when the building was operated by Iraqi personnel. We were sitting quietly on post one evening when, suddenly, Metallica played over the PA. It was awesome. After a while, the watch officer found out what was going on and made the corporal turn it off. It was great while it lasted and was enough to boost the happiness of all who could hear it, on our side at least.

Marines told life stories on post to help pass the time. I got to know some of the guys in my platoon better than my own family. Some posts required two Marines, others were meant for individuals. Just to pass the time, we would sing to ourselves. We did other things to keep from being bored as well. To keep from losing our minds, we would play "the name game" with guys on post. It's a game where you say a famous person's name—for example, Brett Favre—and you have to reply with a new celebrity name, using the first letter of the previous celebrity's last name—for example, "Frank Sinatra." The game went on until we ran out of names. You also couldn't use the same name twice or you lost. We'd share our favorite foods, movies, songs, and stories from childhood. We got good at talking to the darkness of the city as the Marine in the post with us looked out the other direction. If it was night and we wanted a cigarette, we'd take apart an AR magazine and slide the cigarette into the area where the spring had been. This would allow us to smoke a cigarette without having the red glow of the cherry lighting up our post. Most of us needed to smoke so we could stay awake during post, curb anxieties, and be ready for the next attack. The Government Center was a great place to fight from.

Starry Night

At the Government Center, the insurgents were always testing our lines as well as attempting full-on attacks. Two of our Marines were on post one night and received one of these attacks directly on their position. Both had their helmets off, and one was in the middle of eating an Otis Spunkmeyer muffin. He decided to shove the entire muffin in his mouth instead of dropping it and letting it go to waste as soon as the rounds started impacting their post. They both returned fire as soon as they could get their weapons to their shoulder. That's when the radio traffic began.

"This is post Kilo. We're taking a lot of rounds!" the other Marine shouted over the radio.

From my post, I could see the commotion on their post, which was below me and to the southwest, about seventy-five meters. I got out of my small post and stood on the top of the Government Center roof, where there was a short sandbag wall around the top. I rested the bipod of my SAW on the sandbags and took aim in front of post Kilo.

"Kilo, this is post Delta. Where are they shooting from?" I asked.

"Down the road, they're coming from the south," the Marine shouted.

The enemy was really laying accurate fire down on them. Amid the Marine frantically answering my last call on his radio, I could hear the bullets impacting their post. I took my sights and aimed at where I thought the enemy was standing. I let an eight-round burst go out of my SAW and waited. The firing had stopped. It was silent. Within seconds, the fire picked up again, and once again, I let another burst out of my SAW. This time, I held the trigger longer and swept my sights back and forth and up and down around the area. I watched as my tracers danced around the street and off the buildings near the enemy. As the radio call came over, we heard the other Marine's SAW unleash one long machine-gun burst.

"I think you got 'em," the Marine said to me.

"SOG, this is post Kilo. I think they're taken care of," the Marine reported.

"Roger, post Kilo, I'll be up there in a minute," said the SOG. He was making his way to post Kilo to check on the men. A few moments later, we all heard a long burst from the SAW, and I confirmed it when I saw the tracer rounds leaving post Kilo and impacting the area I was shooting at earlier.

"What's going on?" the watch officer asked over the radio. "Who's firing?"

"Uh … watch officer, this is post Kilo. The guy was trying to move, so we shot him."

"I thought you said he was down."

"Um, I did say that, sir, but, uh, now he's down."

Moments later, another transmission came from post Kilo.

"Watch officer, this is SOG."

"This is watch officer."

"Roger, uh, the guy is now on his knees and seems to be praying. I'm going to engage him one more time with my ACOG [Advanced Combat Optical Gunsight] to be sure he's down."

The watch officer interrupted the long pause by saying, "What's going on down there, seriously? I'm coming down there!"

A single gunshot left post Kilo.

"Watch officer, this is SOG. He's down. I shot him in the head."

"Are you sure this time, SOG?"

"I'm sure."

The next morning, my squad ventured to the location where the guy was shot to see if we could recover any intel. Charlie Company had already recovered the body a few hours after we shot him, but there was a bloodied, long-sleeved button-up shirt left behind and one bloody sandal. When I picked up the bloodied shirt and held it up to the sky, it looked like a starry night. The shirt had so many bullet holes, I don't know how the man stayed alive for so long.

Later, when I discussed that night with the two Marines from post Kilo, they were amazed at the significant impact my engagement with the enemy had. They both said that when I fired my first burst, my rounds impacted directly in front of the enemy. "When you fired, it kicked up all the debris and dust from the road. It was really smoky. Then the guys walked through the smoke and began firing again. It was just like the movies. It was crazy."

My firing had allowed the Marines enough time to aim their sights down the road and find the enemy. My second burst hit all around the enemy. I'm not sure if I hit them or not. All I know is that I bought the post Kilo guys enough time to hit the insurgents with their rounds. Overall, it was a good night as no Marines sustained injuries.

Nightmares

Some nights we'd wake up while at the Government Center and frantically search for our weapon. Most guys went through some sort of nightmare, needing to be calmed by the guys sleeping next to them. We'd wake from a dream and not have a clue where our firearms were. We always kept the weapons beneath our cot, where we placed them before bed. My friend Morgan usually slept near me; he always made fun of me for having weird dreams or not being able to find something when I woke in a cold sweat. He laughed because I would never put the boot bands, bands that bloused our trousers up to look squared away, in my boot. I'd spend minutes looking for the hair-tie-sized accessories in the gear that surrounded my cot.

"Shores, why don't you just put them in your boots like everyone else?"

"Maybe because I enjoy searching for them every morning when I wake up."

He'd laugh and tell me I was an idiot.

I had some of the most vivid and violent dreams I've ever experienced while in Ramadi. I wasn't the only one. Many times, my friends would wake up crying, or they'd be sobbing in their sleep and we'd have to wake each other up. I hated hearing my friends crying in their sleep because I could only imagine the horrors that filled their dreams.

The worst dream I ever had was while I was at the Government Center. I dreamed my little brother, only 12 years old at the time, was coming out to see me in Ramadi. In my dream, we took our platoon to pick him up from a warehouse-type place, where he had to slide down a baggage claim to get to our location. He slid down the metal drop and we hugged. It was a great feeling. I remember it felt so good to see someone I knew and loved so much in the dream. I showed him around the city and we went back to the Government Center, where he was going to visit us for a short time. While we were there, a firefight broke out. We had been hanging out in the "dungeon," as we called it, or the lower part of the Government Center where we staged for patrols. I had to leave my brother to go to the roof and help shoot at insurgents. Reports surfaced that Nazi soldiers, of all people, were attacking the Government Center, and they needed everyone with a rifle up there to support the assault. I told my brother to stay with Doc, and Doc said he'd watch him and keep him safe. I went to the roof and killed waves of Nazis as they tried to enter the Government Center. The Nazis were firing volleys of rockets while explosions were happening all around me. We finally killed all the Nazis, and I ran down the stairs to see my little brother again.

When I reached the dungeon, I saw a bunch of guys circling around something. I pushed through the crowd and found my brother burned beyond recognition. Doc was holding him and kept saying sorry. Down on my knees, I cradled his burned corpse. Tears streamed down my face. I felt empty. I didn't know what to do. In my dream, I was crying uncontrollably.

That's when Morgan woke me up. I woke and found myself sobbing. Tears were really streaming down my face. Morgan asked if I was okay, and I told him I had a terrible dream. I wanted to call home and ask how my brother was, to be sure he was okay. I just wanted to hear his voice. Morgan put his hand on my shoulder and told me it was going to be okay and that he was sure my brother was okay. Being that it was only the beginning of our four-day rotation at the Government Center, I drove myself mad wondering how he was for the next three days. When I returned to Hurricane Point, I called home and talked to him. I didn't tell him about the dream. I was just so relieved he was okay and that I could hear his voice. War had found a way to creep into the moments that were supposed to be peaceful and restful. It was seeping into every aspect of our lives.

Contractor

Many times, different units from the coalition would use the compound as a rest stop and temporary staging area while they were moving throughout Iraq. We'd be told not to shoot a specific-colored vehicle as it pulled through the gate because it was full of Americans. Once inside the compound, Iraqi-looking men would get out and walk inside where they would take off their armor-plate carriers and set their weapons down, items hidden beneath their local civilian clothes. A few times, the contracting company stopped by to take care of whatever it was they were doing. During these times, some of their employees would come up on post with us. They always had extremely nice gear and were fun to hang out with. I met a couple of interesting people from these private military companies. One really old guy (old compared to us young Marines and sailors), probably in his late fifties, talked with me on post for over an hour about how he had been a part of the start-up of one of the US Special Forces units. He carried around a PKM machine gun and was one of the coolest guys I had met there. A certain old-surfer vibe emanated from him. I felt at ease because of how comfortable he was in Ramadi. It was cool to see we had guys like him on our side.

Another guy that talked with us had been bragging he was going to go check out one of the posts that sat on the front side of the Government Center. We had warned him not to go up into the post because we didn't have anyone up there. Unlike the rest of our posts, this one lacked protective barriers like sandbags or bulletproof glass. We also reminded him it was midday and that he would be better off checking it out in the morning or late evening when there was less chance of an attack. He dismissed our warnings and insisted he check out the post. His unwavering confidence that he would be fine, coupled with his arrogant demeanor, really bothered me. His assessment on that post couldn't have been more incorrect.

Upon walking up into the post, he paused for a short time before being hit in the neck by a burst of machine-gun fire, which then pinned him down. The insurgents fired so much accurate gunfire into that post that it took 30 minutes to get a medic up there to assess the man's injuries. His contractor teammates were frantically running around trying to get to their downed comrade. We had every one of our machine guns on the north side of the building, firing into the city, trying to find the location of the enemy. We were also lobbing our 40-millimeter high-explosive grenades out into the city, but to no avail. The enemy still returned fire and pinned down that contractor team. By the time a contractor medic could reach the downed man, he had expired, and it then became a recovery effort. When the firefight ended, we watched from our posts as they carried his lifeless body down the long cement staircase to their waiting black Suburban. I am sad for the loss of that American but grateful for the lesson I learned that day. The bigger your head gets, the easier a target it becomes.

The Hole

A piece of myself died alongside Cannan and Mortenson, lost forever. Call it childhood innocence or a new birth into life as a warrior. Whatever it was, something changed in me. I began looking at the Iraqi people as animals and compared them to the feral dogs that roamed the streets. I would sit on post and hope someone would do something that would warrant a death sentence. One less person roaming the streets was, to me, one less threat against US forces. One Iraqi man always walked by my post carrying a black plastic bag and a cell phone. He'd look up at me as I was looking at him through my binoculars. My gut told me he was a bad guy. I wanted to kill him so bad. I was so convinced he was an enemy that I once drew a picture of him while on post so I could show the other Marines what he looked like, somehow justifying to myself and those around me that it would be okay for him to die. I would see him turn the corner, and I'd exit my post and watch him over the sandbag protection with the binoculars.

"Hey," I would shout.

I'd wait for him to look up at me, seeing me gazing at him with the binoculars.

"Fuck you!" I'd shout when I saw him looking up at me.

I'd flick him off and spit in his direction. He would produce a huge smile and continue walking, as if he knew I couldn't do anything about him being there. I wanted to kill him so badly, though he did nothing overtly to warrant being killed. My anger toward the Iraqi people only worsened as the civilians would attempt to convince us there were "no Ali Baba Ramadi" while we were out on patrol.

Every time I heard that, I wanted to cut the tongue out of the individual so they couldn't continue to spread the bogus lies to the next Marine unit. The opportunity for revenge against the local's ignorance, which I felt plagued the Iraqi population, presented itself while I was on post at the Government Center.

I was sitting on one of the posts with another Marine, that overlooked an intersection, just off Route Michigan, which was already beginning to fill with the vehicles of civilians driving to work and beginning their day. The post stood about fifteen feet above the road. I sat in an old office chair, looking to the east out of a bulletproof window that was taken from a Humvee's windshield. The other Marine on post with me looked out to the west. We sat back-to-back and watched as the local populace began their morning in Ramadi. Our command specifically told us any unauthorized people inside our perimeter wire were to be shot. Signs posted in Arabic cautioned death, and there were layers of defenses, including barbed wire, concertina wire, and concrete barricades, to keep unauthorized people out.

Seemingly out of nowhere, an old Iraqi man appeared near my post within the third layer of barbed wire, nearest our inner wall. Grabbing my squad automatic weapon (SAW), I stood up from my chair and carefully placed it on top of the sandbags that sat on the bulletproof window. I extended the bipod of the weapon forward, causing the short barrel of my weapon to rest an inch above the sandbags. I called to the Marine next to me, who was a veteran of the Fallujah battle the year prior.

"Someone's in the wire."

I felt the adrenaline dump as I realized this terrorist would not live to destroy any Marines. The Marine on post with me told me to wait. He wanted to call the situation in and wait for orders from the watch officer. Via the radio, he notified we had an individual in the wire. Other posts confirmed they had eyes on the individual as he wandered about in the wire, carelessly like he had stumbled into the area. He walked out toward the road and grabbed the second layer of barbed wire. He pulled on it with both hands, maybe trying to see if he could get around it and get out, though I wasn't sure. The man looked around as he stood, holding on to the wire. I desired to remove him from this world, just like my two brothers, Cannan and Mortenson, had been removed. Remove him, just as we had been authorized and encouraged to do for anyone trespassing in the perimeter of our compound's barbed wire. No word had come back yet from the watch officer, other than his standing orders that anyone in the wire was to be killed. It was my turn to decide.

"Hey, stop!" I yelled, in both English and Arabic.

The old man looked up at me, still holding onto the wire. His facial expression showed confusion. Blood pumped through my veins, my teeth clenched and my hearing deafened with the whooshing sound of the blood traveling to and from my brain.

"I'm gonna shoot him," I said to the Marine next to me.

"Wait, let's see what the watch officer says," he said sternly.

"No, I'm shooting. He's in the wire. We have our orders," I said, as my face pressed against the cool steel tube of the collapsible butt stock of my weapon.

My sight alignment and sight picture were perfect. I tracked the man with my sights as he let go of the wire and turned around.

"Stop!" I yelled again, in both English and Arabic.

I focused on my breathing as I stayed on the man with my weapon's sights. He was now walking toward the next line of defense, a ten-foot concrete barricade. I pulled the trigger and let a burst of approximately eight rounds leave my chamber and impact around the man.

He immediately danced in place, bringing his knees to his chest and pumping his arms as if that would help the bullets miss him. I realigned my sights on the man and fired a second burst as he tried to move toward the concrete wall. He danced again, but this time he did not walk the same when my firing stopped. He was in pain and was gripping his side. I had also kicked up a lot of dirt from the sandbag because the muzzle blast from my weapon tore a hole in the bag under where my weapon was resting. I quickly fanned my hand to clear the dust from my sights.

The man had made it to the wall, but I could not fire because of another post being beyond where my bullets would impact. I kept my weapon on the man and watched as he continued to grip his right side with his right arm leaning against the wall, left arm above his head on the wall supporting his weight. He stared into the concrete, as if he were wishing he hadn't come to the Government Center that day, as though he were thinking about what was going to happen next. Then, he looked up at me, and his eyes pierced my soul, leaving an eternal void. It seemed like an eternity that the man stared at me and I stared back, begging me to answer one question. "Why?"

Keeping my eyes on him, I told the other Marine to give me the radio.

"What the fuck, dude? You should have waited," he said as he handed the radio to me.

The old man was still looking at me. We were staring at each other as I spoke over the radio.

"Post Seven, this is post Lima. Do you see the individual I just shot?" My friend on another post replied he had seen him.

Post Seven was located on the top of the Government Center, about one hundred meters from my post, and another 50 meters from the main road. The man was now walking away from me along the concrete wall, limping as he held his right hand against the wall for support.

"The man is walking your way, Post Seven. You should have eyes on him in a few," I said over the radio. "I can't shoot because Post Hotel is in my field of fire."

The man walked under Post Hotel, which was about fifty meters from my post. He didn't know what was waiting for him as soon as he broke the protection of the concrete wall that was keeping him from the view of Post Seven. I watched as the man walked away, most likely thinking he was going to live because I had not fired again in his direction.

"You shouldn't have fired, you should have waited," the Marine on post with me said again as he looked over my shoulder at the man.

I still had my sights on the old man just in case he moved back out into my field of fire. I watched as the man limped away, walking to his death.

Post Seven fired one shot from his AR. The man's head snapped back, and he fell backwards. He fell as though he were a rag doll, crumpled into a pile on the ground. It looked so unnatural. The man did not move. I felt disappointed that I wasn't able to finish what I had started, that I had caused him to suffer. I watched as a couple of Marines walked outside the wire to retrieve the dead man from the streets and bring him inside our wire.

As I was relieved from my post after my six hours were up, an officer questioned my shooting. He asked why I had shot. I stood there and talked to him as the dead man lay between us in an open body bag. I remember thinking he looked a lot smaller than I had thought he was. He also looked to be in his sixties. I killed him because he was in our wire. That's what the standing orders stated. That's what I did. The battalion wanted an investigation into the events, so they did not drop it there. A Judge Advocate General (JAG) officer sat down with me and questioned me about the events that had taken place. He asked if I told him to stop in Arabic. I said I had told him to stop in both English and Arabic. He asked me the reason for the shooting and I informed him of the order to shoot anyone within the wire. The JAG officer thanked me for my statement and I left the room. I heard nothing about it ever again, but I think about that old man every day because I know if I had been in the right mindset, I might not have shot him. Upon reflecting on it, removed from the carnage of war, the immediate deaths of my friends, who knows what other decision I would have made?

An officer pulled me aside again after my talk with the JAG officer and told me I was messed up and that I should not have been screwing around on post. He told me I should have been paying better attention. He expressed his disappointment in me.

I realize he may have had the perception I was not attentive because the week prior to the shooting, he caught me on the same post with my eye protection off my face, cleaning my dirty fingernails with a pocketknife. During this situation, he had walked up behind me and immediately began telling me I was a poor Marine for not paying attention while on post, and he was hell bent on making sure I'd get punished for it. He made sure I stayed busy while off my next post rotations by building a fire ring out of small bricks around our massive burn pit at the Government Center. The fire ring made the burn pit look nice, so I'll give credit to the officer for envisioning a way to make improvements.

Everyone did something like that on post at some point. It is nearly impossible to sit and stare out of a window for six hours and not get distracted by something. For me, it was that my fingernails were dirty, so

I thought I would clean them. Yes, it was not what I should have been doing while on post, but I don't believe it gave the officer the right to accuse me of being a bad Marine. I'd like to have seen him stare out the small window under the same conditions and not become distracted.

It was this nail-cleaning incident that caused the officer to continue to ask me what I was doing before I shot the man. I told him I was looking out the window. I told him the man had most likely wandered over to the road that was perpendicular to the main road and walked under our post in the dead space (space that cannot be viewed from a fighting position due to terrain or obstacles) along a concrete wall. There was a small break in the wire near that point, and if no one had stopped the old man at one of the other posts, he could have easily walked without being seen along the wall and out toward the main road where I saw him and killed him. But the officer had a hard time believing me. He didn't like the fact there could have been a break in the wire, especially because he was partially responsible for ensuring the security of the perimeter wire. He hesitantly let me return to my platoon so I could try to enjoy the remaining hours of my rotation off post. The next day he came back to my post and told me there was no way the old man could have walked through the wire. When I looked where the break in the wire used to be, it was now built up and reinforced. Someone must have been busy fixing the small gap while my platoon was off post. At least no civilians might wander into the wire anymore, and no Marine would have to second guess their decision.

Horseplay

Even with the fog of war wearing on us, we found small things to make us smile, ways to have fun. We would wrestle, joke around, and play pranks on each other. Some guys liked to empty half a cigarette, put gunpowder from a rifle round into the center, and then pack a small amount of tobacco back into the end that gets lit. The prankster would give it to someone and eagerly watch as they lit the cigarette. The key was to not make a big deal about having a smoke while trying to keep your eyes on the person with the gag cigarette. Within three drags, the cigarette would disintegrate into a ball of fire, accompanied by a look of terror on the poor recipient of a good joke. We would do this to our own Marines and to the local Iraqi police and soldiers. We always had something to lighten the mood.

One night in the commons area of the Government Center dungeon, my friend, Lance Corporal Young, snuck up behind me and put me in a choke hold.

"What are you going to do now that Marty's not here to watch over you?" he said.

Marty Mortenson was Eric Young's best friend. They had both served together throughout their deployments with Alpha Company, from the invasion through Fallujah and on to Ramadi. Both had been great mentors to me throughout our predeployment training and barracks life. But, returning to the headlock I was in, following Young's taunting comment, I cracked a small smile and simply took a knee. While I knelt down, I grabbed on to Young's arm and rolled my shoulder forward. Little did I know, I had nearly mastered a counter to a rear choke, swiftly flipping him over my shoulder and on to his back. I stood up and smiled.

"I'd probably do something like that!" I said, as the others from my platoon cheered on and laughed.

But our laughs soon dimmed after we realized he was on the floor, writhing in pain and holding his shoulder.

"Dude, I think you seriously fucked me up!" Young complained.

We all gathered around Young to see what was going on. That's when we saw his misshapen shoulder. I must have looked like I saw a ghost. I felt sick and realized the world was going to crash down on me for injuring a fellow Marine while horsing around. Immediately, all the Marines stood around and argued over who knew how to best reset a dislocated shoulder. Next came the arguing to decide who should give it a go. I stood back, sweating and feeling ill. I just kept apologizing. Doc Lake went and grabbed his med bag as Young begged for pain relief. The corporal who helped fix things at the Government Center had convinced everyone he would be the best at resetting Young's shoulder, so we all watched as he gave it a go. Although Young preferred to wait for pain relief before any intervention, the helpful corporal successfully persuaded him he wouldn't need it once his shoulder was repositioned. Young gave in and allowed the helpful corporal to have control of his arm. Young groaned as the corporal placed his foot in his armpit and pulled slight tension on his arm.

"I'm pulling on three," the corporal said.

"One, two ..."

"Fuck!" yelled Young.

The corporal looked as though he was going to pull Young's arm right off. He gave one good pull and gently let Young's arm go. His shoulder still looked deformed. By this time Doc was back there with his med bag, Staff Sergeant "Papi" Santiago was also there, wondering what was going on. He did not look happy.

"Shores, what the fuck?" he asked.

I told him we were just messing around, but then he pointed out something that hadn't crossed my mind.

"What are you gonna do when we have to call a medevac for his dumbass?" Papi sternly asked.

I hadn't thought about that. My heart dropped. I felt even more sick. I hadn't realized how bad it really could be if we couldn't fix his shoulder.

"Give him the pain med and give it one more shot, Doc," Papi ordered.

Doc pulled down Young's pants to expose his butt cheek.

"Put it in the smiley face! Give me the shot in the smiley face tattoo, Doc!" Young pleaded.

He had a tattoo of a yellow smiley face on his butt cheek, but Doc didn't want to put the morphine in the tattoo. We all laughed as Young got loopy on the morphine. He was laughing and kept calling me an asshole for ruining his body. Once the pain went away, Doc gave one more go at resetting Young's shoulder. The second attempt failed to work, and his shoulder remained dislocated.

"I have to let the LT know," Papi said. "We need to get Young to a doctor."

I was done. I was convinced I was going to get a non-judicial punishment, the military equivalent of a misdemeanor, only worse as it typically dropped us in rank which in turn dropped our pay. The lieutenant (LT) came down and was quite disappointed. He called for a medevac to come from Hurricane Point. It was another platoon, and I knew then that one of the most feared staff sergeants was coming.

He was a miserable man, the most feared in the company by us junior Marines. He would get angry out of nowhere and explode. When I first arrived at Alpha Company, I ran into him when I was leaving the company office. I had been talking with Maynard, another new Marine, in the company office and was leaving when I ran into the staff sergeant just outside the door.

"Good morning, Staff Sergeant," I said with a smile on my face.

I was happy to be there with Maynard, who was in my School of Infantry class. Maynard and I had just been joking around as I left the office.

"Wipe that fucking smile off your face," he barked with his lips pursed tightly and his tone scolding and disgusted.

I immediately didn't like the guy and did everything in my power to avoid him. Rumors spread that he was at the Government Center with his platoon when Iraqi citizens began massing outside one of the gates. He went down to help with crowd control and decided the Marines needed to fix their bayonets to their rifles. Most platoons, including ours, fixed bayonets on their rifles at times due to the proximity of people near us while we patrolled the souk. I vaguely remember this as I was a SAW gunner and didn't carry a bayonet.

The crowd continued to grow as the platoon sergeant stood out with them and demanded the mass of people to back up. One aggressive Iraqi man got close to him and he bayoneted him in the stomach. He and one other Marine from another platoon, during a different altercation, were the only two I knew of to have used their bayonets against an enemy in Ramadi. He was an impatient and angry man, and now it was my turn to feel his wrath.

Young was all bandaged up and ready to move once the other platoon arrived. While we were waiting, our LT pulled me aside and asked me what happened. I told him that Young had come up behind me and asked what I was going to do now that Marty wasn't around to help me. Our LT recognized we all were still grieving Mortenson and Cannan's deaths and understood we weren't intentionally fighting or anything.

He told me not to let it happen again and made sure that I understood I could have been in a lot of trouble, but he was going to do his best to keep me from that. As I left the room, I felt ashamed and guilty for putting other Marines in harm's way. I sat with Young and awaited the arrival of the other platoon. When they arrived, their staff sergeant stood at the entrance to the dungeon and talked with Papi. I watched from afar, attempting to read his demeanor and awaiting my fate. He was in his full combat gear and looked like he was on a mission to find me.

"Where's Shores?" he yelled. I stood up and walked up to him.

"Here, Staff Sergeant," I said as I nervously stood at parade rest.

He walked right up to my face. "You realize that I could have had my Marines injured because of this? How would you have felt if we would have been blown up and someone would have died for this? You fucking idiot. You better pray nothing happens to us on our way back to the FOB."

"Aye, Staff Sergeant," was all I could mutter.

I felt bad. I hadn't thought through of any of those things and, worst of all, I could see the fear and concern for his men in his eyes, that he might lose someone over a dislocated shoulder. I hoped nothing happened to them; I was ashamed to put all of them in that situation. Despite how the staff sergeant reacted, I hoped everything was going to be okay and that he didn't hold any grudges. I would have felt the same had the roles been reversed. I listened to the battalion radio while they mounted up and departed to take Young to the next level of care, to make sure the platoon arrived safely. Fortunately, everything went well and Young was back with us in a day or so.

I don't know how I would have reacted if someone had been hurt because of my mistake with Young's shoulder. It was hard enough to hear about people risking their lives for us to have some level of comfort or mail delivered.

Some of the Marines who died during our deployment weren't even recognized as part of a fighting infantry unit. We had Marines, whose military occupational specialty was cook, die bringing hot food to Hurricane Point. We could have done without the convenience of hot chow, but the cooks did their best to make sure we had it. Some died so we could have watery eggs and undercooked bacon. The mail service Marines succumbed to the same fate to bring us letters from home.

After that incident with Young's shoulder, I always gave that staff sergeant more grace when having to deal with his lack of patience. I somewhat understood why he was always upset. I'm sure I wasn't the first 19-year-old he'd had to set straight for acting like a kid. It's a relief nothing happened to that platoon during their transport mission for Young because I don't think I could have forgiven myself.

RIP (Relieve in Place)

Throughout August, our battalion continued taking casualties and, when September came around, it was finally time to begin our rotation home. Our last couple of patrols were meant to ensure a smooth turnover and area familiarization alongside 3rd Battalion, 7th Marine Regiment (3/7). We had some of the leadership from the company that was to replace us with our platoon during this time. We would be in areas that were used by insurgents for ambushes, and the lieutenants from the other battalion would ignore our advice about the best practices when patrolling the town.

"Sir, you don't want to take a knee here," I warned one of them.

He looked at me and remained on his knee, as the rest of us kept in constant motion to keep from being an easy sniper target. I said nothing else to him as it was obvious, in his mind, that he knew more than a lance corporal. I figured he'd learn the hard way, or one of his Marines would. Combat allows no room for arrogance or ignorance.

I had never thought I'd leave Hurricane Point alive. While sitting outside our hooch, smoking and playing guitar, we saw a gunnery sergeant ("Gunny") from 3/7 walking through a field, roughly fifty meters from us, toward 4th Platoon's hooch. The sound of incoming mortar rounds ripped through the sky moments before impacting the field between the Gunny and our position. Combat had worn us out so much that we remained smoking our cigarettes, paying no attention to taking cover, while we found amusement in the Gunny's dive to the ground. There were no more mortars, and we watched as he picked himself up and dusted himself off. He said nothing and we only waved when he looked in our direction as he stepped it out to 4th Platoon's hooch.

Our movement back to Camp Ramadi to begin our return home felt as though it would never come. We believed karma would take our lives before we left the country, and most likely during the movement back to Camp Ramadi. We spent a couple of weeks stationed there, during which we cleaned our gear, loaded company equipment onto shipping containers, and relaxed. I spent a lot of time watching movies with others, watching movies by myself, reading, and reminiscing with friends. We had our combat deployment debrief from one of the chaplains. "Now gents, when you get home, don't go and take out your anger on your family. You can't be hitting your wife or your kids. Don't get too drunk and say stupid things about this deployment. People don't want to hear about the gruesome details of what happened. Don't be picking your nose in front of people. You're not going to have those hearty Iraq boogers anymore. If you need to talk when you're home, be sure to contact me."

We all laughed it off and thought he was a joke. The last person any of us would have wanted to talk to was him. We didn't want to confide in anyone who didn't understand what we went through. In our eyes, he was a personnel-other-than-grunt (POG) who didn't understand combat.

On Camp Ramadi, we'd go to the chow hall just to watch the female service members walk through the line and sit down. We weren't really making any sexual comments about the women or anything like that; it was just that, for the past seven months, we really hadn't seen an American woman in person. We would catch each other stumbling over sentences or pausing in the middle of a sentence when we'd look at them. We'd laugh it off and continue on with what we were doing or saying. Though we knew we were much safer on Camp Ramadi, we'd still get harassed with indirect mortar and rocket fire from the insurgents.

I was in the shower trailer one morning, near our barracks. They were nice compared to the ones we had back at Hurricane Point; they had heated water. It was nice to stay in the shower for a little longer than we had at our FOB. I was washing my hair and had my eyes closed when I felt the trailer tremble from the overpressure of a rocket that had just passed over the shower trailers. The rocket passing by knocked the soap off the tray; it landed on the shower floor. I stood there scrubbing my hair. In that moment, I didn't think about my family or friends. In that second what crossed my mind was, "Damn, I hope I don't get blown up in this shower because I don't want one of those pretty base women to see my blown off, lifeless, flaccid penis, or even worse, have to pick it up. That would be embarrassing."

What I failed to realize in that tenth of a second was that it wouldn't have mattered because no woman would have wanted to have sex with my dead body regardless of whether or not I were naked, but my 19-year-old mind went to the same place most men my age thought about.

I didn't die from that rocket, but a Marine from 3/7 did. He was walking out of the chow hall and was on his way back to the barracks. The rocket hit directly in front of him. My friend and former roommate, with whom I had served in Ramadi and, later, the 31st Marine Expeditionary Unit and, finally, combat in Afghanistan, was just exiting the chow hall. The Marine from 3/7 disintegrated right in front of him. Army soldiers spent the next couple hours securing the site and picking up the Marine's remains, placing him in black bags to be identified. He had just arrived in Ramadi. What a place.

The Trip Home

Going home was the best feeling in the world. I knew my family would be waiting for me at Camp Pendleton. We all talked about what we were going to do when we got home. Some of us were going to go out and find the biggest burger place. Others wanted a steak. I wanted some good pizza and some beer. I also had a craving for fried onions and green peppers, of all things.

Getting on the last plane home seemed to take forever. We experienced a ten-hour delay for our plane from Kuwait. We all sat on the buses near the airstrip in Kuwait, waiting for our plane home. I chose to lie under the bus, where the luggage is usually kept, so that I could stretch out my long legs and relax. During that time, I must have listened to the new Gorillaz *Demon Days* CD that I had bought at the PX at least ten times. I had almost memorized the songs by the time we were boarding the plane for our flight home.

That plane ride home was exciting. I didn't sleep the entire flight; it didn't help that there wasn't much room for me to get comfortable, but I was just too giddy to get back to America. I stayed up and talked with one of the flight attendants in the back while I drank freshly brewed coffee. Everyone was giving me hell when they walked by.

"Hey, Shores, can't you wait another eight hours to get some pussy?"

"Come on, Shores, you have a girl waiting for you already."

But I wasn't interested in any of that. I was tired of sitting my extremely tall body in a cramped airplane seat with other Marines and gear. Back by the flight attendants, I could stand up and lean against the wall of the plane, drinking as much coffee as I wanted. I was also trying my hand at pretending to be as normal a person as I could be. I most likely failed miserably, but what better way to try than on someone I'd never see again, who was keeping me supplied with fresh coffee.

When we finally arrived, I was sick with excitement. I wanted to fast-forward my life to the point where I was hugging my family. The past seven months had led up to this point, and I couldn't believe I was finally here, alive. My family, along with all the other families, had been there since eight in the morning. It was now around ten in the evening. They, too, had to wait for our delayed flight. We drove by the groups of waving friends and families as we first had to turn in our weapons into the armory. Only then could we march up to where our families were screaming for us. The Marines who were 120-dayers, like Eric Young and others, were there to meet us with cans of beer and drunken smiles. We had to march up to our families in formation, while our Marine brethren who had been out of the Marine Corps for a couple of months stuffed our cargo pockets with cans of beer. They were drunk, stumbling alongside our formation and yelling for us. Guys were beginning to cry, others were chugging the beers while marching in formation on our way to see our families. We made our way to the top of the hill where we could hear the cheering from our families. It was around eleven at night and, fortunately, the organizers brought in portable lights with generators, so our families and friends didn't have to sit in the dark while waiting.

An orange glow from the halogen lights appeared as we neared the top of the hill toward the parade-deck staging area, showing a mass of people waiting for us. We marched up to the crowd, who were now close to the formation. Crying mothers and fathers, wives and sons and daughters, brothers and sisters, all surrounded our now smothered marching formation. We all did our best to maintain the integrity of our ranks and ourselves, but eager wives and mothers didn't seem to care about the formalities of the formation or the Marine Corps. They wanted to hug their son, to feel the life that still graced their bodies. Goosebumps spread over my skin as I listened to the screaming women, the shouts of relief from parents and spouses. It overwhelmed my senses in such a way that I couldn't control, almost like I had smelled something extremely spicy. My sinuses opened up, and I did my best to choke back the tears, that feeling of relief that I was home. A sense of panic filled me. I saw my family; they were jumping up and down, covering their mouths in excitement. It felt like a dream, with my heart beating so fast that it could somehow stop. Believing I didn't deserve to return home, I never thought this day would come. I had convinced myself I was never coming home again, that I'd never see the smiles on my family members' faces. That I would never experience the smell when I hugged them, their tight hug of reassurance that everything was going to be okay. But that evening I felt those things and couldn't have been more grateful. An indescribable feeling accompanies coming home from combat that can only be experienced. If only for a moment, the feeling of serenity and peace can bring the hardest warrior to tears. It took me a good while before the tears stopped streaming down my cheeks.

CHAPTER 7

Continuing to Serve

The New 1st Platoon

After the deployment to Ramadi, several changes took place for the 1st Battalion, 5th Marine Regiment (1/5). First, we found out upon our return that there wasn't space for us on Camp Pendleton. So, they placed us in old Quonset huts from the Korean War era. The camp where we were stationed served as the filming location for the movie *Heartbreak Ridge*. The place was run down, lacking any heat or good insulation inside. Winter was just beginning, and several of us were freezing. Not the welcome we had expected.

Second, Alpha Company went through significant changes. Because of the losses of Marines from casualties and from those who reached the end of their service contract, our company was short Marines. Our command had to split up platoons and move Marines around to fill staffing needs. Also, because several of the Marines in each platoon were originally specialty trained to operate crew-served weapons, they had to be reassembled into a contemporary weapons platoon. All the movement of personnel led to mixing of personalities and some bumping of heads from previous quarrels between platoons. I remained in 1st Platoon, but I got separated from most of my close friends who were assigned to other platoons, specifically, Arnett, Morgan, Garcia, and Tager. From our platoon, only Mark Albert and a few others remained. The new 1st Platoon absorbed the Ramadi 4th Platoon. We gained some solid combat veterans from the move. However, we lost our solid platoon commander and platoon sergeant. In their place, we had a new second lieutenant from Quantico as our new platoon commander and a former drill instructor (DI) as our new platoon sergeant. I did not like the platoon sergeant's idea of leading Marines. He was a nice enough guy; he was just stuck in the DI mindset. Also, there was a camaraderie between the existing 4th Platoon members which made it difficult to break into the friend groups established during the Ramadi deployment. To top it off, a number of the Marines in the company, who had been in the battle of Fallujah and Ramadi, made it known that Fallujah, in their mind, was a more important deployment than what had just taken place. Ramadi was an improvised-explosive-device-ridden city of death compared to the conventional warfare that took place in Fallujah, and there was a feeling of disdain put forth by those who had participated in both deployments. No one wanted to talk much about Ramadi; when the senior Marines did, it was only to say it was a terrible deployment compared to the initial invasion or battle of Fallujah. It left several of us whose first deployment was Ramadi feeling like outcasts and the bastards of the company.

I had first met our new platoon sergeant while I was in boot camp. At the time, he was a Marine Corps Martial Arts Program DI. While I was in line at the chow hall in my third phase of boot camp, he jumped in line to grab his food. This was a typical practice, as the DIs were busy and had to eat and get ready for their next period of instruction. However, the thing that separated him from the other DIs was what he said to me. He looked at me as he cut in line and remarked, "I'm going to cut in line. If you have a problem with that, I'll roundhouse kick you in the throat." I looked at him and replied, "Aye, sir."

It was comical, and I thought little of it. However, by the time I had been with the new platoon sergeant for a few months, the boot-camp antics were not amusing and I hated being around the man.

Alpha Company also received several new members to our battalion, who had combat experience from other units within the Marine Corps. One of these people was a salty soon-to-be corporal. He was quiet but carried himself well and was a solid Marine.

We began preparing for the workup for the next deployment after establishing the new platoons. We were going to be deployed to the Pacific Theater as part of the 31st Marine Expeditionary Unit (MEU). It excited me that Alpha Company had always trained as a boat company when not doing back-to-back desert deployments. Our duties would be littoral raids and spending copious amounts of time on Zodiac rubber boats. But first, we all had to go on 30-day postdeployment leave to rest.

My fiancée and I married while I was on leave in October 2005. I wore my dress blues for our wedding and the ceremony went well. A number of family members and close friends made the food for our wedding and provided a lot of support for our marriage. My wife was only 19 and I had just turned 20; a lot of our peers had doubts about the success of the marriage. I knew it was what I wanted and needed for my life, so I didn't think much of it. My wife, however, took a lot of criticism from her peer group as she had just graduated high school earlier in the year while I was in Iraq. Even while she was finishing her senior year and I was deployed, teachers and friends told her she was too young to marry. But she stuck with me. I love her for that and so much else.

Many of our friends attended the wedding, which had upwards of two hundred people. This made for a shitshow of a reception with underage drinking and looks of horror from the teaching staff of our high school who were attendees, as they drank alongside many of us. It should be noted that, in the state of Wisconsin, you can drink underage if you have a parent present, so this was fully embraced for the evening. It wasn't the classiest event as my wife reminds me from time to time, but it sure was a celebration; for that, I'm left feeling content.

I spent a lot of time with family and friends and truly appreciated the time I had at home while on leave. It was exciting to have been married as well because my wife was planning on moving out to California with me. That meant I could live off base and not have to spend any more time freezing in the Quonsets. We were looking forward to the drive across the country, back to San Clemente to settle into our new, tiny apartment.

Once 1/5 returned from postdeployment leave, we hit the ground running. That year, we attended the Marine Corps Ball in Las Vegas, and

I had the honor of being chosen to carry the flag for the fallen Marines. I remember practicing the ceremony with all of the command-level officers of 1/5 out in the parking lot during the weeks leading up to the ball. It was a cool experience for a lance corporal as I was seeing the other side of the Marine Corps, our garrison traditions. Carrying that flag was an honor. I recall some of the office staff officers sort of chuckling to themselves as I walked the flag out because I was so serious and rigid. Not that I was nervous; it was because the act of carrying that flag felt so heavy on my heart from the losses earlier in the year.

After the ball, our command sent me to Infantry Team Leader's School, and we began snapping-in, or preparing for our annual rifle qualification. I had shot expert in boot camp and I wanted to maintain that certification. After early mornings on the rifle range, I left with another expert badge. After we completed the range and team-leader's course, they sent us to specialty schools to support the littoral mission ahead of us. I chose to go to Assault Climber's School. Other options were coxswain's course, scout swimmer's course, and maritime navigation. I liked the idea of learning to climb mountains and rappel, so it was a simple choice for me.

Assault Climber's School was an intense, two-month program where we learned how to scale a cliff face in different environments, establish climbing lanes for the rest of our Marines, and evacuate wounded. It was a great course, and it concluded with us climbing at Joshua Tree National Park, one of the best areas for lead climbing in the United States. We also learned how to scale buildings with special equipment and rappel down the side of buildings and into rooms. My friends also joined me on the course, so it was a great chance to build rapport with them prior to deploying.

Two of my close friends and I were the team leaders for our squad when we returned to 1/5. Our squad leader, Sergeant Mark Albert, was a solid addition to complete an amazing team. We were the only four combat veterans in our squad. The rest of the Marines in our teams were "boots"; this was going to be their first deployment. We spent the remainder of the workup to deploy training as a company. Our first company training was to be down on Coronado Island to learn about our Zodiac boats and how to properly conduct a beach assault.

We left for Coronado as a company in early February. It was miserably cold. We spent a couple of weeks learning how to function as a boat company. During that time, we'd spend countless hours floating out on the ocean. Some of our Marines' bodies couldn't hold up to the elements and they went hypothermic, having to get pulled onto a safety boat and warmed up. One time we returned from being on the ocean all day in forty degree overcast weather. My fingers were stuck in the grip position as I had spent most of the day holding the ropes that line the gunnel tubes of the Zodiac. Large swells had tossed us around, with nothing for us to do except hold on tight the entire time. I remember standing in the warm shower that evening with my eyes closed, feeling as though I was still rocking back and forth with the ocean, and painfully opening my fingers so they could attempt somewhat normal function.

The ocean is a brutal place when you experience it beyond its beauty from shore. I remember standing on the deck of one of the large landing craft that transported our company with our Zodiacs, being tossed about by the ruthless swells. Our company gunnery sergeant ("Gunny"), who was in Ramadi with us, and his boat crew launched first from the landing craft to check the swells. When the ten-ton gate closed after they departed, I watched out the bow of the craft, seeing the sky, then coming down a swell to see the next wave. The gate would almost scoop the next wave like it was ice cream and douse us with seawater, only to pitch up to the sky for the next one. The safety boat called back over the radio, stating it was too rough to launch the rest of the company for our training raid. We then had to recover their boat back onto the landing craft so we could return to base. The ten-ton steel gate dropped to allow for the Zodiac to beach itself onto the deck of the landing craft. We watched in terror as the swells caused the large gate to pancake the water as the coxswain and Gunny tried to time their boarding. Had their estimates been off as they barreled toward the landing craft, the gate would have squashed the crew underneath, killing them. Lucky for all of us, the timing was impeccable, and we cheered as the Zodiac shot onto the landing craft, just in time for the gate to pancake the wave behind them. My hat goes off to the SEALS and others who spend their military career on the water, cold and wet. It's a grueling undertaking, and the effects it has on one's mind and body are nothing to take lightheartedly.

After our training at Coronado, we began our standard infantry tactics and maneuver training. We learned to work together as a unit in order to operate effectively in the Pacific region if deployed to combat. They told us we would be leaving in July and stationed at Camp Hanson on Okinawa. Just before our predeployment leave, I received a promotion to corporal. My wife and my friend and mentor, Sergeant Albert, pinned on my rank for the ceremony. After that, my wife and I packed our belongings and drove back home to move her back with her parents for my deployment.

Oki, July 2006–January 2007

We arrived on Okinawa and went right into more training evolutions. The ocean was much prettier and more pleasant to be on than it was in California. Countless evolutions were done in our Zodiacs, training to assault beaches. Additionally, we received training in non-lethal techniques for crowd control and restraint. We had to be sprayed with oleoresin capsicum (OC), basically pepper spray on steroids, which was just terrible. I asked a friend of mine who had been shot in the leg if, given the choice, he would prefer being shot or being sprayed with OC. He replied with no hesitation that he'd wish to be shot again. As someone who has never been shot, I can only describe being sprayed with OC as one of the most unpleasant experiences. After our certification in non-lethal hand-to-hand and OC, we cleaned ourselves up and prepared for an evening of non-lethal weapons training on the range. While we were on the range in our riot gear, sweating caused the OC to reactivate for many of us, resulting in being taken off the range. For a moment, several of us were wincing and trying to effectively shoot our firearms, as the OC reburned our eyes and skin. It was hilarious.

We did a fair amount of jungle-warfare training throughout the northern part of Okinawa. We spent a little over a week up in the northern training area where we practiced patrolling during the day and night through the triple-canopy jungle. The jungle was so dense that our night-vision devices didn't work well as there wasn't much ambient light. We had to rely on holding the Marine's shoulder or gear in front of us as we stumbled through the relentless terrain.

I was navigating for our patrol one night. This meant I was second in line and held an iridium-lit compass to lead the way. The Marine on point in front of me was roughly five-and-a-half-feet tall and wiry. We moved through the jungle, and I was constantly looking down to be sure we were on the correct heading for our objective. I felt the leaves from the trees brush by my face as we walked through the vegetation, never knowing what was brushing against me. We were all terrified of the venomous spiders, snakes, and centipedes in the jungle. We were always on the lookout for the large banana-spider webs that caught birds. The spiders are the size of a large man's hand. Unfortunately, I happened to have a run-in with one of these spiders on this particular night patrol.

As we paused the patrol to ensure we weren't getting too spread out, I noticed one of the leaves I had just brushed past was still on my face. I used my right hand to brush it away. But when I reached up with my hand, the "leaf" twitched and grabbed on to my face. That's when I felt the legs that were attached to it and realized an enormous spider was covering my entire face. I panicked and reached under the body of the spider to pull it off. As soon as I began to throw the spider off my face, it attempted to hold on, scraping at the skin on my face with its long legs. It then bit me on the joint of my right thumb, tearing my skin as I blindly launched it into the jungle. When the spider was out of my hand, I gasped, realizing I had been bitten. I called out, "I'm bit!" One of the Marines behind me said, "What'd you say?" I called out again, "Something bit me!"

I have never seen Marines care less about a training mission and break light discipline, scrambling to turn on their white lights. As the blood drained from my thumb, I gazed around to witness Marines dancing with knees high in an attempt to locate the spider. One of them shone their light on my wound and called for our doc. The doc put a tourniquet on my right arm, just above my elbow, and told me we had to get to the battalion aid station (BAS) as quickly as possible.

When we arrived at the BAS, a medical officer greeted us. He looked over my bite and told me I was lucky the spider bit me where it did. It seems I was fortunate enough to avoid the spider's venom, as its fangs merely tore my skin instead of delivering a true bite. Had it injected me with venom, it would have been a different story. I thanked everyone and left with a bandage and some ointment.

After completing some other patrols and the infamous obstacle course, we returned to Camp Hanson. Our command set up a tour of Shuri Castle and a few other historic landmarks that we visited as a company. It was an honor to step foot in the places the Marines before us had fought in World War II. During the tour, we explored the caves where the Japanese engaged in combat and took their own lives, and observed cliffs where civilians chose to end their lives after being deceived by their government regarding the treatment they would receive if captured by US forces.

After several Marines made poor decisions out in the village of Kin, located just outside Camp Hanson, which caused the rest of us in the battalion to have our liberty privileges revoked, it was time for us to get on ship and explore the Pacific. We boarded a Navy amphibious assault ship.

USS *Juneau*, LPD-10, was an amphibious transport dock, commissioned in 1969 and eventually decommissioned in 2008. The interior and accommodations on board reflected its age, but the crew did a good job keeping it as clean as possible. Our berthing area, where we spent most of our time, had tight quarters with sardine-like sleeping racks. I wondered how I was going to fit in a bed with such little room because, if I lay on my back, I would be longer than the bed. I ended up securing a top bunk since it didn't have a top covering it, just miscellaneous pipes from the ship running overhead. This way I could lie on my back and bend my knees up, straddling some sort of pipe with my kneecaps. I was happy because it was about as comfortable as I could get without being an officer or sailor.

Once we left the shore power at the dock on Okinawa, the ship really showed its age. The air conditioning only worked intermittently and the exhaust system was sub-par. The smell of diesel fuel and exhaust was always present, mixed with saltwater and sweat while underway. I felt sticky and grimy in the late summer heat while we traversed the Pacific Ocean. While on ship, we would train on infantry weapons systems and do our best to keep in shape with physical-fitness training. We also fired our weapons off the rear of the ship a few times to keep up our marksmanship with close-quarters battle drills. Our job was to be ready to assault a beachhead with our Zodiac rubber boats, so we trained to prepare for that. We did a few training missions where we left *Juneau* in the middle of the night to assault a beach.

I was feeling uneasy the first time we departed the well deck while the ship was still underway. The back of the ship had a massive steel gate that dropped to allow us to move down to the black ocean. Sailors stood by with life-safety devices should something happen while we prepared to launch. When it was my boat's time to launch, we carried the heavy Zodiac, weighed down with our firearms and gear and a 50-horsepower motor, down to the ramp. Other than red and green lights from the ship, we had little to guide our way. I remember looking out to the black ocean with nothing in sight and seeing the seawater churning violently from the ship's wake. It appeared the water was pulling at anything near the edge of the ramp, waiting for someone to slip so it could pull them into the dark abyss. We all wore personal-flotation devices (PFDs). However, I can only imagine we would die from thirst before someone discovered us floating in the middle of that dark ocean.

My boat launched just fine as we made it out of the ship's wake and into the emptiness that exists in the middle of the ocean at night. We were able to meet up with the rest of our element, and the coxswain began circling as we waited for the rest of the company to launch. Once we were all launched and watched the ship disappear into the night, we began our movement to land. I did not know where we were going and was thankful we had a couple of boats with navigation equipment. The droning sounds of the boat motors, coupled with breathing the exhaust fumes, was always disorienting when everything around us seemed flat and black.

As we neared the shore, we saw lights from what appeared to be a village. As we came closer, though, something felt off. Just offshore, three people were huddled together, wearing nothing but underwear, while several others who were clothed stood on shore and faced them. It crossed my mind that we might be encountering some kind of crime or torture. I soon realized as we debarked that our training mission had us assaulting a military base of some sort. I found out later that the men in the water were candidates for the Philippine sniper program and were being hazed by their instructors.

We dragged our boat to shore and readied our equipment for travel. It was still early in the night, maybe around midnight, and we still had our mission to carry out. We moved through the dense jungle and up to our objective. Another platoon was on the objective, which was some sort of retrieval of information. The situation was chaotic and made clear to me the importance of understanding the mission. Our command during this deployment did not do a very good job of passing along the information for what we were going to be doing and what our objectives were. Our behavior reflected this, as we all kept asking where we were going and what we were doing. We were good at setting up in patrol bases and maintaining our security, which is what we did while the officers figured out what was going to happen next. After spending some time there, we made our way back to the boats.

Finding a spot to sleep was necessary as the ship wouldn't be back for us until later the next morning. That our command allowed us to sleep casually without worrying about combat security made us happy. We still had Marines awake with fire watch to guard our weapons and gear, but it wasn't as vigilant as it would have been in a combat situation. We spent the night on the dark beach and woke up to paradise.

The cove we awoke to was beautiful. We made our breakfast with the MREs (meals, ready to eat) we had packed and relaxed as we waited for the ship to come back for us. Some Marines were already trying to open the coconuts that lined the shore, some nearly cutting themselves with their feeble attempts. Many of us swam out into the cove and, inevitably, we began to wrestle and indulge in horseplay. Some Marines hopped on other Marine's shoulders and fought others in the water. It was a lot of fun.

Soon enough, the ship returned. We dragged our boats into the beautiful blue water and returned to the steel prison that was USS *Juneau*. We cleaned our firearms of the salt that had accumulated on them and prepped our gear to be ready for our next mission.

Tug-of-War

We had a successful remainder of the deployment, with several other Marines being promoted to corporal. We traveled to the Philippines, where we did some training with Philippine Marines and left there for China. Apparently, we were the first Marines to have trained with the Chinese military in something like fifty years. We prepared for some friendly competitions, like a shooting and obstacle course. They selected some of us to play basketball and take part in a tug-of-war against Chinese soldiers. Because I am very tall, they chose me as one of the Marines to play basketball and join the tug-of-war. I had zero interest in playing basketball.

When we got off the ship to go to the basketball game, we drove around the mainland for a bit, taking in the sights of China. We arrived at the gymnasium to find nearly every Chinese soldier was, conveniently, as tall, if not taller, than me. Needless to say, we didn't win the basketball or tug-of-war games. Their best soldiers were sent to beat a group of Marines who had been stowed away on a ship eating sub-par food for the past few weeks. After the competitions were through, we could go back to the ship to change into civilian attire so we could go out on the town. I enjoyed what I saw in China. We dined at a restaurant and went out for drinks. It was fun, and I enjoyed the experience. When it was time to leave, we headed back toward Okinawa so we could wrap up the deployment.

We discussed and made plans for what would come next in our time in the Marine Corps. My two good friends and I discussed the possibility of going to a new unit called Marine Special Operations

Command, or MARSOC for short (now referred to as "Raiders"). The opportunity arose for us to go there as they were looking for combat veterans willing to join the unit. The catch was we each had to pass a professional-development course to move to the unit, and we had to extend our time in the Marine Corps.

Opportunities

I had broached the subject of extending my time in the Marine Corps with my wife, who was not pleased to hear but understood. Her only request was that I not reenlist, and I agreed. Between the three of us combat veterans who were considering extending our contracts, I was the only one who was married. When we all returned from our postdeployment leave from the 31st MEU, we had to decide if we were going to extend and go to MARSOC. Both of my friends were second-guessing their decision to extend and wanted to get out of the military. I had made up my mind and expected the other two were still on board. I felt as though I still had to earn my life, through the process of going back to war again. Ramadi had such conflicting scenarios that I felt compelled to go back to make things "right." One afternoon, while the three of us walked up to the chow hall on base, I asked them, with a sly grin on my face, "How would you guys feel if something happened to me, if I extend and go to MARSOC, and you guys didn't?"

That was enough of a strong-arm to change their minds. They both called me an asshole for putting that on them, but they agreed that extending for the experience of what MARSOC had to offer was going to be worth it. Our invite to joining MARSOC hinged on each of us having to complete a training course. My requirement was successfully passing the rigorous Infantry Squad Leaders Course (ISLC). It was a grueling three-month school focusing on the skills needed to lead infantry Marines in combat. There were a number of solid Marine instructors and students attending the course. At the end of the training, I was honored to receive the recognition of Instructor's Choice, the Marine recognized as the one who the cadre would like to serve alongside in combat. It was an honor but I was bummed I wasn't able to receive the Meritorious

Mast certificate in person at the ISLC graduation ceremony as I had to return to MARSOC to begin our training.

Upon graduation of the ISLC, I joined the rest of our new platoon at the range where we trained in close-quarters combat and room clearing. From there, we went up to Bridgeport, California, for mountain-warfare training exercises. My wife and I made the decision to move her back home to live with her parents since my extensive training schedule meant I would rarely be present. We found ourselves on ships, on helicopters, and working from vehicles, learning a crash course of unique skills to support our next mission. We conducted live-fire training raids, live-tissue medical training, and survival, evasion, resistance, escape training. The whole experience was a blur as we worked our way up to the deployment, which was supposed to be Iraq. We found out a week prior to leaving, however, that our orders had changed to go to Afghanistan.

Before departing for the deployment, which technically formed part of the 15th MEU, my squad got chosen to travel to the Philippines and deliver a month-long course to the Philippine National Bureau of Investigation, Drug Enforcement Agents, and special forces. SEAL and Green Beret teams previously conducted the operation, known as *Leather Piston*. My squad, along with our platoon commander and a small group from headquarters, lived in the city of Tuguegarao for the month, traveling from our hotel to the small police base just outside the city, to conduct the training. By the end of the course, we had nearly eighty students running live-fire drills through shoot houses our platoon commander had designed. We were proud of them; it was rewarding to see their growth in skills and attitude as we came to the end of the training. After the month ended, we traveled back home for a week to ready our gear to head to Helmand Province, Afghanistan. My wife flew out to see me in California for that week. We spent as much time together as we could, though I was busy getting gear and personnel lists packed and ready for our next stop. Saying goodbye as I dropped her off at San Diego International Airport was difficult as I now knew what combat was and knew I was possibly not coming home the same person. I stayed in line with her while waiting to go through security until it was her turn to walk through the checkpoint. The escalator was close by her checkpoint so I got on it and let it slowly take me down. I turned and we looked at each other for as long as the descending escalator would allow. I was choked up but don't recall any tears this time. I was focused on the mission ahead and knew I had men relying on me to bring them home safe.

Afghanistan, January 2007–June 2008

My deployment to Afghanistan was the last thing I did in the Marine Corps. It was the best deployment and I couldn't have been with a better group of guys. Our training made us highly effective in combat. We were professionals. I extended my time in the Marine Corps to deploy to combat again, as I needed to redeem myself to God, my country, and myself.

I had earned the rank of sergeant while training for the deployment, serving as a squad/team leader and stand-in platoon sergeant. My position within our unit for that deployment allowed me to help my Marines make better decisions than I had in Iraq. The success in the leadership of our platoon and company in Afghanistan was because of the experience of the men who had been to combat in Iraq.

For the men I served with in MARSOC Bravo, thank you for everything. It feels good to come home from a war and not doubt our actions. I contemplated writing more about this deployment in this memoir, however, I feel it would take away from the message and experiences I needed to convey in this book. I may write a follow-on memoir of these experiences because they were unique and amazing in their own ways and I would want to do justice to those Marines and sailors from the first Bravo Company. I'm proud of what we accomplished there, and I have no regrets about the enemy we killed. In my experience, no regrets should follow the killing of someone who is trying to kill you. I am proud to have rid the world of some well-trained Taliban combatants. They were outstanding fighters compared to the insurgents in Iraq, and the combat was the closest thing to conventional warfare as we could get in the War on Terror. Emptying a B-1 bomber on Taliban who were littering the mountains, throwing hand grenades at the enemy, and clearing out trenches was the stuff infantry Marines yearned for and I am fortunate to have experienced and survived. We located, closed with, and frequently destroyed the enemy. The Taliban were well organized and trained, but the Marines from Bravo Company caught them off guard. While serving in Afghanistan, I was recommended for combat meritorious and meritorious staff sergeant, which deservedly ended up going to someone else. Despite not being promoted to staff sergeant until my return from Afghanistan, I took pride in being considered for the meritorious promotion. I also had no intentions of reenlisting as I was looking forward to starting my new life outside the military, so a meritorious promotion was better suited to a lifer. I found the offer of a $90,000 tax-free incentive to reenlist into MARSOC intriguing, but I firmly believed I had exhausted my fair share of luck and that the money was not worth it. My wife would have also left me, which would have sent me spiraling into darkness as she was my rock and support, having dated me since I was 15.

I felt odd leaving MARSOC, as it was a place I felt comfortable. I was finally where I felt at home and effective as a Marine. We fought in combat the way it should be. It was the "Wild West" when we were in Helmand; most of the members of Bravo Company would agree it was one of the best deployments anyone had been on. We only had two major casualties. While engaged in a gunfight, a close friend of mine sustained a gunshot wound to his leg and, in a separate incident, a member of 1st Platoon suffered an arm injury from a mortar round. Some others had small shrapnel wounds, but nothing that took them out of the fight to be sent home. It was incredible to me, having seen the type of combat fought in Ramadi, that our circumstances were so fortunate. Though it was tough to leave MARSOC, I felt I had redeemed myself to God and to the Marine Corps by serving my last tour in combat. We were winning when we left. I also want to give a very special thanks to all the policy makers from the United States Government who put their hard work and sweat into the disaster of a withdrawal from Afghanistan that was finalized in August 2021 (just kidding, fuck you).

CHAPTER 8

Home

Society and War

War is more than a battle between two nations. It is more than a fight for an ideology. When you take part in war, it becomes a battle to save your own soul. It is a battle to keep yourself from falling into the dark abyss of hatred that makes life easier as a combatant. Easier to hate all the noncombatants, the women, children, and elders. Perhaps it is easier to accept that God doesn't exist as no God could desire the acts of war upon its own creation. Easier to accept that, no matter what happens, you may die in a foreign country and not even understand why you were ever there.

Accepting my death in Ramadi, Iraq, proved to be a mistake that brought many regrets I will carry for the rest of my life. As I experienced, when I lost track of my soul and when I accepted my death, I became the enemy. I turned into a terrorist in a foreign land and displayed little mercy toward my opponents. It was not until I returned from war and saw what I had at home that I realized what we had taken away from so many people—family and friends.

As Marines, we're taught to improvise, adapt, and overcome—principles that are ingrained within us throughout boot camp and our career as one of the few who earn the title of "Marine." Our training instills the mentality to push past any emotion that could hinder the completion of a task, stressing the importance of perseverance in the culmination of success and the accomplishment of a mission. We do not become brainwashed while attending boot camp—our minds just get cleansed of all the political correctness and passivity our Western society infuses into us throughout our young, privileged lives. During boot camp, we learn to trust our instincts and embrace the fears warfighters face. Gavin de Becker's book *The Gift of Fear* is a brilliant example of how our society teaches us to go against our gut instinct. To become an effective warfighter, we have to understand fear. As Americans and members of Western culture, many of us consider the things so-called Third World countries do as savage and disgusting. It seems farfetched that, in some countries, corporal punishment is acceptable. We as Americans have the luxury of ignoring these events.

I've had conversations with several people that would jump at any opportunity to mold today's wars into a logical sequence of events. Some wars in the past have not needed explaining. People understood what the mission of the military was. There was an identifiable enemy, an identifiable goal. Many of Western cultures have learned from their mistakes and have since attempted to find more civilized ways than war to deal with political issues.

I often encounter a sense of disbelief when I talk with someone about the events of war—almost a hesitation to believe the kind and cool-mannered individual standing before them took part in combat. Ask any self-identified "patriot" what they think should happen to terrorists and almost every answer will include death. It rolls off their tongue without hesitation and without a true understanding of the enemy. In my experience, death breeds death. We kill one of theirs. They must find justice through killing one of ours; the cycle continues. We can and must do better.

We blame religion and are quick to justify our actions on behalf of our God. When examining Islam, the religion of many of those we fought in Ramadi, I often recall what the angel Gabriel said to the prophet Mohammed in the first contact that was made with him. Gabriel told Mohammed, "Read!" All of us could learn much from this interaction as reading is one of the most powerful tools we have as humans. Yet, many of the extreme followers of Islam believe in following only what is written in the Quran, with a focus on taking action against nonbelievers.

This same doctrine applies to extreme followers of Christianity (or any religion for that matter). In both religions, a person could handpick a surah or verse to justify the murder or oppression of another. That said, a majority of the followers of each religion still choose to seek more information through reading and choose peace as their path.

In learning from others' experiences, we can deepen our understanding of the world. Nowadays, all people seem to do is watch—watch social media, watch others' opinions, and take them for truth. Each of us has a role in improving our understanding of our enemies' viewpoint through self-education, primarily through reading. Perhaps our enemy has been oppressed their entire life, led to believe it's our fault. It's our duty to prove them wrong. Just because a terrorist takes the life of one of our citizens doesn't mean the rest of the people associated with their religion or race have the same extreme ideology. We can and should do better as a society. It starts at the level of the individual and must remain peaceful so as not to lose our civilized way of life.

The Marine Corps strips young American volunteers of their privileges, of the comforts of living in Western culture, and prepares them for the hardships and reality of the other side of the world. We must understand our enemies in order to be effective warriors, or diplomats, in today's wars. I use the word "diplomat" here because the wars we fight now aim to "win hearts and minds" rather than attempt to measure success through the number of dead or miles of ground gained. This concept became clear during the war in Vietnam; our leaders are still trying to perfect it, if that's even possible. Unfortunately, Iraq was the major recipient of the transition from conventional ground warfare to the "three-block war" concept.

Conceived by a Marine general in the late 1990s, the concept of a three-block war is conducting combat operations on one block, conducting peacekeeping on the next and doing humanitarian aid on the last. It focuses on training the members of the military to conduct all three sequences at the same time to allow for the most efficient use of the military. It is important to put a focus on the leaders of military units at every level, specifically the "strategic corporal," or the lowest-level noncommissioned officer in the military. By enabling the lowest level of leadership positions to create an excellent base for implementing the three-block war concept, we can reach the strategic goals. To make this concept work, we need to provide enough time and resources for the training of these lower-level leaders. The Marines of 1st Battalion, 5th Marine Regiment, had insufficient training and resources, which manifested in the three-combat tour men in Ramadi as hate and self-preservation from combat fatigue. That fatigue seeped into the minds and actions of the junior Marines.

Many of the leaders of our company and platoon were salty combat veterans. They had firsthand experience of being fired at, killing enemies, and taking part in large-scale missions during the initial occupation of Iraq. Our company and platoon comprised many veterans who also had firsthand experience in the Spring 2004 Fallujah battle, where civilians were given the ultimatum to leave the city or be treated as enemies. The Marines had fought block-to-block, house-to-house, killing everything that got in their way. Command told them anyone remaining in the city after the evacuation was to be considered an enemy. From the stories I heard from many of them, this was true. There were no "hearts and minds" to gain; it was a conventional ground battle. After securing the city, they fulfilled their mission, concluded their tour, and returned home. They were rewarded for their efforts with only a short six- or seven-month break, much of which they spent on combat training in the field for the next deployment. Many of these men were between the ages of 20 and 25 but, to young Marines like me, they might as well have been 50 years old. Wise and battle hardened, they were the old men of the Corps, having seen the true brutality of humankind. Their faces looked young, but their minds and spirits had grown old in a short time. Missing in them were innocence and hope—qualities we junior Marines still carried. This innocence is not recognized as missing until the new troops or people back home begin pointing out ways the veterans changed after only seven months of combat.

When I see a burka-clad woman here in the United States, or an Arab family walking around, I don't get anxious, like many people think I might. I don't have a hatred for them; they are just trying to live their lives in a country that promotes freedom. I commend them for having the courage to be proud of their religion and heritage in a country that, many times, frowns upon the very fact they are even "allowed" in. Bad people can be found everywhere, in every country. We seem to need an enemy though, and, unfortunately, many from the Middle East are the recipients of that hatred. I hope people can forgive my actions in Iraq for decisions I made as a teenager. If anything, the fact the American media tried to justify that we did anything "good" over there brought more harm than good. In my experience, I believe we shouldn't have been there in the first place. Special forces have been trained as professionals with solid target packages and limited combat exposure to the civilians of the country they are operating in, and they are prepared to fight the current wars against insurgencies or guerrillas. The response should not be to flood a country with young, trained killers full of naivety who will do anything to come home alive.

The American news networks have talked in the past about "tragedies" that occurred during Operations *Iraqi Freedom* or *Enduring Freedom.* They showed the American public everything, from videos of Marines urinating on dead Taliban soldiers to photos of Army soldiers posing with dismembered bodies. Our government is concerned the leaking of these photos and videos into the hands of the enemy could be used as propaganda against coalition forces. Books like E. B. Sledge's *With the Old Breed* discuss moments when Marines urinated into dead Japanese skulls. These actions aren't unique to our culture or times. They are what war does to people—people who, in other circumstances, would shun such behavior. The genuine hatred that comes from the civilians of countries we occupy stems from the poor decisions teenaged American troops, like me, make that take something away from the person, whether it's a family member, friend, or something as simple as their dignity or what little freedom they have. We have to be better as a society and as a fighting force. We need to talk about what war really is. We need to discuss the grotesque display of humanity that is war, not just the bombs and the money we send to support ourselves or other nations. If we forget it, we repeat it. We must acknowledge it. Unfortunately, as of this writing, I'm seeing similar actions being taken by combatants for Israel and Ukraine, countries the United States has supported financially and militarily. We need to be holding these countries to our standards. The first step is to provide an example of what we expect of our allies. We can and need to do better. The genuine tragedy surrounding the wars we fought in Iraq and Afghanistan is that they left all of us who fought on "our side" wondering, "What was our purpose?" The failed withdrawal from Afghanistan was a concise way of showing what the War on Terror was. As a ground-fighting Marine division, I ask, what did we accomplish there? The politicians send us to war and expect us to abide by our standards. When the enemy doesn't abide by the same standards, where does that leave us? At a loss. We cannot fight an ideological war with smiles and candy. War must be fought brutally and quickly, or we should not participate. If war is the last option, then we have exhausted all except the brutal killing of the enemy and anyone who supports them. I fear that Americans have become more focused on armchair-quarterbacking actions that took place in combat so "justice" can be served rather than doing their own research into the brutality of the Islamic State to their own people. We see one side of the war as civilians: what the media shows us.

Wanting to share with others what we have accomplished is in our nature. We cry out when we see photos of our military members posing with the dead men who tried to kill them, yet we applaud the hunter who poses with the dead body of an animal. There is no greater feeling of accomplishment than killing someone who was trying to kill you. Hunting wild game doesn't come close to the feeling of killing an enemy combatant. Surviving is an amazing accomplishment, which is why people will pay thousands of dollars to experience adventures that risk their lives, to get to that core feeling of survival. Several men I served with are avid hunters; I am by no means discrediting hunting. It's just that, for me, war changed my desire to go sit in the woods, hunting game. I can probably just attribute that to sitting on post at the Government Center and promising myself that I'd never sit and wait like that ever again.

War is a drug, no different from caffeine or alcohol, and it alters your mind. When the adrenaline pumps through your body nearly every day, over the course of a combat deployment, you look for the next high. Combatants do not differ from drug addicts when it comes to searching for that next high. We have to recognize this effect so we can do better when we enter the next war. We have to do better for our children and for our country so we don't create more enemies.

For the soldiers or Marines who have not yet been to war, here is some advice: don't take photos of the carnage. What happens over there is difficult for people back home to comprehend. They haven't had the adrenaline dumps and the horrific experiences that diminish the previous terrible ones. They won't understand how the photo of the brains sitting in the back of a sedan is funny. Don't set yourself up for failure and take photos or videos of these things. If you survive the combat, those mental images will haunt you for the rest of your life. Trust me, it's hard enough to process those. You don't need physical images to linger. One of the worst parts about war is surviving and having to make sense of the nonsense war is.

As of 2025, it's been 20 years since I was in Iraq. Twenty years of figuring out what my purpose on this earth is. I still have not found a definite answer; I doubt I ever will. Some days are better than others, and I find telling the difference between either type of day has often been difficult. I have noticed my tendency to explain to people I just met that I served in the Marine Corps, as if I'm trying to notify them before they label me as damaged goods. I feel like I'm different from them, that they need an explanation for why I am the way I am. I'm not looking for pity, I'm searching for someone to understand me. It was tough watching the drawdown of troops from Iraq, wondering if we helped over there. I watched in the news as my boot-camp senior drill instructor, Staff Sergeant Moncie Johns, was killed while working as a civilian contractor in Basra on June 17, 2014. I was upset with all the confusion about what was going on and, in 2015, I attempted to raise money on GoFundMe so I could go fight ISIS overseas. After only a few hours, GoFundMe flagged my fundraiser and denied it for its failure to abide by their policies. Fate had different plans for me. Fighting ISIS wasn't one of them.

One word sums up my experience of leaving the active-duty military and returning home: loneliness. I found it was tough for people to understand what I had been through. Once people discovered my veteran status, they felt an urge to recount a story of someone they knew who had encountered combat. I understood they were trying to relate and be respectful, but it was extremely frustrating for those first few years. The US personnel who fought in Ramadi have been in some of the toughest combat. Not because the act of shooting someone is difficult—at least for me it wasn't. It was the mental strain of wondering if the actions we were taking were the right ones. It was the act of having to determine friend from foe, all while taking friendly casualties and being told to win hearts and minds. Being exposed to that nonstop for seven grueling months wore down everyone involved. It made it difficult to express those feelings to the people back home when they think war is as simple as what the movies make it out to be. The loneliest part of being back home was that I didn't have any way to express the confusion or the thoughts that clouded my mind. At least when I had been surrounded by my Marine brethren, we had a mutual understanding of each other's feelings. Family and friends back home felt foreign.

Experiencing combat in both Iraq and Afghanistan has allowed me to prioritize what things in my life are important. Instead of pretending everything is okay, I've discovered that telling people what's on my mind is easier for me. It doesn't bother me if people consider me a geek because I have the desire to play a video game, or if they view me as less of a man for crying during a movie. I sometimes have a hard time controlling my emotions; I've learned to accept that. I'm so busy suppressing thoughts and emotions throughout the day that I'll just wear new ones on my sleeve. Certain progressions of music can bring me to tears, and I can't explain why. The first few years after I got out of the Marine Corps, I got good at building walls to block emotions. It wasn't until my wife and I realized that we both needed support that I learned how to break down those walls.

I arrived home from Afghanistan in April 2008 and, within two days of landing in the United States, was at a wine and art show with my wife back in Wisconsin. It was a surreal and foreign place where people were handing out fine wine, bidding hundreds and thousands on locally made art, all while dining on exquisite cuisine from the top chefs in the area. All of this sent me into a panic attack; it was too much, normal. Very few knew where I had been a week prior and I felt so out of place. I wanted to be back with my men and I was mad that everyone seemed so carefree and happy. Didn't they know there was a war going on?

I returned to Camp Pendleton to finish my out-processing and was back home and out of the Marine Corps by late June 2008. Though my deployment to Afghanistan proved to be an infantryman's dream, I still had things I needed to process from the combat in both Iraq and Afghanistan. On top of the stresses of combat, I was still having a difficult time processing the deaths of Mortenson and Cannan. I felt extremely guilty about their deaths and wondered why I was allowed to live. The guilt made me want to numb myself, so I'd drink. I'd drink a bottle of vodka at night and eat an entire frozen pizza. All I wanted to do was barricade myself in my newly purchased house, play video games online with my brother and brother-in-law, get drunk, and eat terrible food. Mentally, I was in a reckless and dangerous place. I missed the adrenaline rush from combat and Marine training. My frustrations with not being understood were showing in my attitude towards loved ones. I once yelled at my mom for touching a belt loop on my shorts when we were going to take a family photo. She had tugged on my loop to pull me in closer to her.

"Let go of my fucking pants," I looked into her eyes and barked.

She looked so hurt. Again, I had hurt one of my parents, who did nothing wrong. I felt so ashamed and asked for her forgiveness. I think she knew I wasn't myself, but that didn't give me the right to treat her or anyone else like that.

In the fall of 2008, I started studying business management at college and also contacted the local veterans' hospital to get mental-health care. I found the students at school extremely frustrating and knew my patience was wearing thin. Their poor attitudes and work ethic made me angry. Many were the same age as me, but I thought they were much younger. My blood would boil when someone would make an excuse for not completing a simple task. I'd want to choke them to death so they couldn't enter the workforce and take jobs from people who deserved them. But, being a good Marine, I maintained my bearing and would remind them they paid for the classes they were now complaining about. I didn't really care for school at first. I wished I were still in the Marine Corps. But, on October 23, 2008, my view of the world changed once again.

A traffic accident claimed the life of my brother-in-law on his way back from school. He was only 17. He and my younger brother were in the same class and were great friends. They had been friends since they were nine years old. I was excited that I would be able to see more of them now I was out and back home. My wife and I were torn apart at the loss of her little brother. I had been looking forward to getting the help I needed for my time in war when the death of a close family member shattered all hopes of putting my own needs first. Being there for my wife and family was crucial.

My inability to be as supportive as I should have been stemmed from the fact that I was still processing my combat experiences. She was my support network when I got home; that went away when her brother died. We couldn't give each other the support we needed, so our relationship started to fall apart. Before my brother-in-law died, I lost my temper a few times, once breaking my hand on the fridge in a fit of drunken rage. The punch disfigured my hand; it is still noticeable. Another time I punched the plaster wall in our house and put a hole in it. We covered it with the famous photo of the sailor and nurse kissing outside in New York after World War II. Oh, the irony.

After my brother-in-law died, I continued to lose control of myself and my emotions. My wife was losing herself, too, and we were growing further apart. My drinking and smoking became worse, and I became numb to the world once again, as I was when I had first returned home from Iraq. I felt her brother had died because of my wrongdoings throughout my time in the Marine Corps, specifically Ramadi. It was my payback from God for what I had done to other people. I convinced myself this was the way it was meant to be and just the beginning of events to come that paid back the things I had done. The understanding I reached was that my purpose and punishment for surviving Iraq was to carry on living as others perished around me. I was in hell and my time there was just beginning. I contemplated walking outside and killing myself. An unfortunate number of times, I've tasted the gun oil on the front of my handgun as I had it in my mouth. Sometimes I would put it to my head just to remind myself that the life I was in was real. Other times I would get so depressed and numb that I would do it just because I wanted to feel something. My life was filled with hatred; being home made me angry. I wanted my friends to be with me. I felt the urge to return to a combat zone. In Ramadi, I had planned to have the death I deserved. I was ready to die in Ramadi. Living life was not what I expected.

On a Halloween night in 2009, my wife and I decided to attend a costume party at a local bar. She was dressed as Little Red Riding Hood and I went as the Big Bad Wolf. I had found a large women's nightgown and was wearing prosthetic wolf face pieces for an awesome looking Big Bad Wolf. We attended the party and were having a great time when something out of the ordinary caught my eye. I saw a Marine I knew wearing his dress blues. I saw nothing but red as my heart began to beat out of my chest. I stopped dancing and made my way through the crowd to confront him. By the time my wife realized what was happening and reached me, I was already yelling at the Marine to leave. I was furious that he would wear his blues to a costume party and, there I was, in a dress, yelling at him. My wife was trying to pull me away from him while she said it wasn't my problem to worry about. But it was my problem and, as I spoke, the Marine realized it was his, too. I told him he needed to leave because it was disrespectful and he nodded in sheepish agreement. I couldn't let it go and mulled over it for days afterward.

In these reflections on life and stressors, it came to my attention there was still a battle to be fought, one that concerned my mind and my soul. I didn't want Cannan, Mortenson, or the others from 1/5 to have died in vain. My life had a purpose, a purpose that surpassed my understanding. I decided I needed immediate help from the veterans' hospital. I called and set up an appointment with one of their mental health care providers. Within days, I was in and talking with a doctor.

The irony of it all is the first thing I saw when I walked into the doctor's office: a photo of a sunflower field, showing flowers as far as the eye could see. I flashed back to the improvised explosive device that killed the five Marines from 2nd Platoon. Blood-splattered sunflowers. The panoramic shot of the sunflower field immediately turned my stomach, but I told myself it was a sign that I needed to be there. The doctor set me up with a therapist, and we scheduled our first meeting. I asked if I could bring my wife with me because I felt we both needed help, with her brother's death still only weeks old. She said it was against the policy of Veterans Affairs (VA) to give spouses mental-health assistance but, given the circumstances, she would do it and we would have to keep it quiet.

Through our almost year-long weekly sessions, Doctor Laura gave both of us the tools to make it through relationship and personal issues. Many of the tools were so basic yet worked so well. Things like asking the other person for a "time out" if our conversation got too heated, keeping it from boiling over. We also learned how being upfront and honest with our feelings of frustration was more effective than trying to ignore them. We also took the time to reward ourselves after our sessions by going out to dinner. It was nothing fancy as we were broke and both going to college, but Perkins Restaurant and Bakery also helped to keep our relationship together, salty shit food and all.

The sessions were like going to the gym in that there would be weeks of significant progress and then a plateau of seemingly no forward movement. Our sessions reached a point where I felt as though my not getting better was becoming frustrating to Laura, and I also became frustrated that I'd have to leave our session when the time was up. It was frustrating that I had to open up so much and then have to leave after unpacking the traumas because our scheduled time was over. I could have talked for hours on those minute details. However, I would have to spend the next week dealing with the feelings brought to the surface, and I was growing tired of fighting them. Therapy is work, there's no two ways about it. I refused to go on medications, as I didn't want to numb my life anymore. As with most things in life, the harder the work, the greater reward upon completion. Were it not for Doctor Laura, I don't think I'd be married, let alone alive. She saved my life and my relationship with my wife, and I can't thank her enough. I am glad to have been through therapy, and I continue to see my new psychologist, Dona, throughout the year. Dona, too, has saved my life by giving me tools that are more effective at life than suicide. I'm beyond grateful for her. She is a miracle worker. It's difficult and frustrating, still to this day, but, for any vets reading this, I suggest you give therapy a shot. It will not fix everything, but it gives you some tools that can help. Small victories. On top of the anger and frustrations I felt, there is a near-crippling feeling of loss that continues to bear on me. It is a feeling of the fear of those around me dropping dead from some random event. Since returning from Ramadi, I've felt the crushing pain of the loss of those closest to me. If my wife doesn't respond to a text or call in a manner that seems reasonable for whatever she is doing, I begin to fear she was in a fatal car accident or that she has fallen victim to one of the many crimes taking place at any moment within the United States. Spiraling out of reason for what could be happening, I imagine my life without whatever person I am worrying about and it sends me off into a dark depression. The minutes turn into hours and I find myself desperately trying to find a reasonable excuse as to why I haven't heard if my family is okay, only to convince myself they are not. So I start grieving for their loss and planning for what needs to get done to exist in a world without them. Deeper down into the abyss of despair, I find myself searching for an answer. It is sometimes so crippling I trigger my sympathetic nervous system into thinking something is happening and I wind up with an elevated heart rate, dry mouth, and a clouded brain where no amount of reason will cure my catastrophizing until I hear the voice of my loved one. It has gotten worse over the years and I attribute that to my unfortunate practice of thinking of the weight of such loss.

When I would attend our sessions at the VA hospital, the psychologist would check in and see how I was doing. I'd fill out the paperwork that asked how I was doing on a scale of one to five. It would also ask if I had thoughts of suicide and, if so, if I had a plan. I always had a plan, and it was always a good one that would work; however, I always lied on the form. I was so worried the VA would deem me a threat to myself or others, and take away my firearms, that I lied. Reflecting on my concerns, I was terrified the doctors would force me to get the firearms out of my house because they had mentioned it as a possibility in a prior session. I relied on those firearms to feel safe in my house. I had survived by having a firearm; they were possibly going to take away the one safety net I had because I had thoughts of hurting myself. That made me feel so misunderstood. I wanted to protect myself and my family for 99 percent of the time; the 1 percent of the time I had thoughts of suicide, I was risking losing the feeling of comfort and security the firearms provided.

I don't mean to undermine the importance of that 1 percent, as I recognize the finality of suicide success rates due to firearm use to be a valid concern. I feel the time I spent fantasizing about killing myself did not compare with the time I spent fantasizing about someone breaking and entering to cause harm to someone in my house. As someone who was almost a statistic myself, I don't want to downplay the significance and impact of veteran suicide. During a desperate moment, I held a loaded pistol to my head while my wife pleaded with me to not end my life. After getting out of the shower, I stood naked and reached a breaking point with whatever situation we were going through. I was caressing the trigger on my .45, leaving fate to see if it was enough pressure from my finger to put the gun into action. It was an intense moment as we were both yelling, crying, and in a state of out-of-control emotions. I was ready to die because I couldn't see how my life fit in with the rest of society. Another time I wrote a suicide note to my family and took several pain killers I had left over from a surgery, mixed with a lot of brandy. I again was leaving my life in God's hands as I went to bed, not knowing if I'd wake up. When morning came, I sheepishly threw out the suicide note, burying it in the trash under the dinner scraps from the night before. These two events happened years apart, before and after my therapy sessions at the VA. In my years of dealing with suicidal ideation, I've come to realize that it ebbs and flows. No matter how much therapy I've taken part in, it's still there. It can come on like a thunderstorm and I only pray that I continue to persevere in fighting the thoughts.

Dealing with stress—not only in combat but also dealing with stress in general—is a key to a happy and successful life. People often try to compare my combat experiences with theirs, saying, "I could never understand what you went through." But they can. After talking with those closest to me, I've come to realize that your worst stressful experience is at the same level as mine. We have experienced our seemingly max capacity for stress with each of these events and have a difficult time coping with them. For some people, it's witnessing a car accident; for others, it's being sexually assaulted. Any event that takes away a piece of humanity, either from you or from another person you are witness to, is an event that will leave a mark on you. It's how we cope with these events that sets the bar for how our life will move on. I've experienced decisions from either side of the bar, and I can tell you that choosing the most difficult direction of healing is much more rewarding than choosing the numbing option.

The thing I've come to realize about war is that the true battle begins when you get back home. You can leave the war, but it will never leave you. The combat deployment was only a prelude to the lifetime of processing that follows. Many people give up on themselves and their loved ones. The combat stressors only amplify as "normal" life stress piles on top of an already heaping pile of shit. Children and jobs add more stress. Choosing to live a life without addressing the stress of combat is like installing a new floor over eggshells. Yes, the floor may look great, but as you walk across it, you will hear all the shells breaking beneath, and so will everyone else. You have to make a choice.

Now viewing life through the lens of a nearly forty-year-old, I reflect on the war I took part in and watch as we near the potential for World War III with the conflicts in Ukraine, Russia, Israel, Palestine, and Lebanon. I look at several teenagers in our society today and wonder if they would be ready to defend our country if war ever came to our soil. The military makes young men into fighting men, and I see it more now than ever when I interact with a 19-year-old civilian or a 19-year-old service member. The amount of responsibility given to an 18- or 19-year-old by our government is incredible when you consider what they are working with. We received machine guns, grenades, C-4 explosives, grenade launchers, knives, as well as thermal and night-vision optics, and we were tasked with defending our country. Some parents have a hard time handing over the car keys of their family car to kids that age. Yet we were and are only capable of making the decisions that our still-developing brain can handle, regardless of training, when handed responsibility. Teenagers made poor decisions. Combatants are teenagers. Teenagers are developing. We send developing brains into combat, where they establish a new baseline to grow from. Our baselines as combatants are much closer to fight or flight, and we establish those feelings as the norm. This is where we veterans get into trouble later in life. We go back to our worst moment and respond to a current event with a similar tenacity. The response doesn't match the situation and the veteran is in trouble with either the law or a friend or family member. Care of veterans means understanding where they are coming from at a primal level, not just paying for and caring for the "damage" that may have happened. We can do better as a country and I challenge our politicians to take this into consideration when writing new policies.

As for work outside of the Marine Corps, I can say I've tried my hand at a number of career fields in an attempt to find the one that fits me best. After I received my associate's degree, I went to a career fair. An event participant laughed at me when I told her I was looking for more of a career than a job, after she asked if I had an interest in working in metal finishing. I found it hilarious when the miniseries *The Pacific* came out and showed one of the main characters trying to find work upon returning from war. He told the lady at the fair that he had experience in killing people; she didn't know what to do with that information. I'm certain many of us grunts from the Marine Corps and Army have shared similar experiences.

I chose to go further than only pursuing my associate's degree and earned a Bachelor of Business Management. I've tried my hand at several industries that fall within that field of study. I'm an entrepreneur, but I've spent my time as a career firefighter, emergency medical technician, private detective, filmmaker, videographer, financial advisor, and blue-collar laborer in metal finishing. I'm always on the lookout for the "next big thing," and those close to me will tell you that my ideas, though eccentric at times, are never lacking. I am a creative at my core and I think this has also helped me address my combat experiences. The Marine Corps built on my already innate ability to improvise, adapt, and overcome. The ability to overcome is the constant of the three traits that we have to be comfortable in addressing year after year.

It's now been two decades since the Ramadi deployment. From the outside, my life looks pretty normal. I spend my days doing work and working on the house. As I cart the kids to their activities with the other parents, we engage in small talk about the weather and what's going on in the world. Unless someone asks or brings it up, I don't talk much about my service. Overall, my life is "boring" compared to my 19-year-old self; I like it that way. Having healthy kids and a safe home for them to be raised in is something I am grateful for. I waited until I was 32 to have children and I'm happy I did. I wasn't ready to have kids until then, as my mind was a jumbled mess and I was trying to figure out who I was. While I acknowledge I will make mistakes as a father, just like everyone else, I can confidently state I have a deeper self-awareness now than ever before, which enables me to provide our children with the attention and environment they require for their happiness. I am grateful to be able to say that, as I know several of those men I served with had young children while trying to address the aftermath of combat. To these men, I say this: you are an amazing father. You did the best you could, as we all do, with the tools you had. I'm proud to have served with you and, if your children are at an appropriate age to read this memoir, I hope it helped them to better understand the things we went through. To those kids, give your father (and mother too, as they are right there with us in the stress of dealing with combat) grace and forgiveness. They were doing their best, and they are good men and women.

In the years since 2005, I've been spotty at keeping in touch with some of the Gold Star family members of Marty Mortenson and Matthew Cannan. Only recently have I had the pleasure of being back in touch with Ken and Ruth Mortenson, Marty's parents. Ruth is an author and has helped me to navigate the process of writing. It was important to me to have her read this memoir in its raw form so I could get the perspective of one of the mothers of the men I served with who died. Ruth has always been a straight shooter and didn't hold back on her thoughts about this memoir. She has also given a lot of perspective and closure to me with the death of her son. Ken and Ruth are devout Christians and I appreciate their perspectives with navigating life. Being in touch with them has been very cathartic. I encourage anyone who has lost a comrade to reach out to their families. It means a lot to them and it can help to bring you closer to the significant memories of the time we have with each other.

A positive mental attitude, therapy, and a desire to push on keeps me going every day. I struggle for days at times, but overall I couldn't ask for a better life than the one I am living right now. Therapy has also given me tools to deal with my everyday life and the new stressors that inevitably come up. I am better at dealing with the unexpected now that I understand more about the human mind and my reactions to these events. I sometimes find myself acting like I'm still in Iraq when I do certain things, such as not waving with my left hand, noticing objects alongside the road, and evaluating everything when I'm outside my house. But I don't want to let my guard down. I've survived being hunted. I don't like surprises, so I'm always thinking about the worst-case scenario. Preserving the things I've learned, which have saved my life in the past, is important. It's important to me that I don't disappoint my Marine brethren. Marines and sailors, like the men from 1/5 (1st Battalion, 5th Marine Regiment) who gave their lives, live on through the stories from us survivors, whether they are good or bad. You can kill a man, but you can't kill the Marine Corps. Fortunately for me, I am a Marine. Make Peace or Die. *Semper Fi.*